Raspberry Pi System Software Reference

Warren W. Gay

Apress®

Raspberry Pi System Software Reference

ISBN-13 (pbk): 978-1-4842-0797-0

ISBN-13 (electronic): 978-1-4842-0796-3

Managing Director: Welmoed Spahr
Lead Editor: Michelle Lowman
Development Editor: Douglas Pundick
Technical Reviewer: Stewart Watkiss
Editorial Board: Steve Anglin, Mark Beckner, Ewan Buckingham, Gary Cornell,
    Louise Corrigan, Jim DeWolf, Jonathan Gennick, Robert Hutchinson, Michelle Lowman,
    James Markham, Matthew Moodie, Jeff Olson, Jeffrey Pepper, Douglas Pundick,
    Ben Renow-Clarke, Dominic Shakeshaft, Gwenan Spearing, Matt Wade, Steve Weiss
Coordinating Editor: Kevin Walter
Copy Editors: Sharon Wilkey and Kim Wimpsett
Compositor: SPi Global
Indexer: SPi Global
Artist: SPi Global
Cover Designer: Anna Ishchenko

Distributed to the book trade worldwide by Springer Science+Business Media New York, 233 Spring Street, 6th Floor, New York, NY 10013. Phone 1-800-SPRINGER, fax (201) 348-4505, e-mail orders-ny@springer-sbm.com, or visit www.springeronline.com. Apress Media, LLC is a California LLC and the sole member (owner) is Springer Science + Business Media Finance Inc (SSBM Finance Inc). SSBM Finance Inc is a **Delaware** corporation.

For information on translations, please e-mail rights@apress.com, or visit www.apress.com.

Apress and friends of ED books may be purchased in bulk for academic, corporate, or promotional use. eBook versions and licenses are also available for most titles. For more information, reference our Special Bulk Sales–eBook Licensing web page at www.apress.com/bulk-sales.

Any source code or other supplementary material referenced by the author in this text is available to readers at www.apress.com. For detailed information about how to locate your book's source code, go to www.apress.com/source-code/.

This book is dedicated to the memory of my father, Charles Wallace Gay, who passed away this year. He didn't remember it when we discussed it last, but he was responsible for sparking my interest in electronics at an early age. He had brought home from his used-car business two D cells, a piece of blue automotive wire, and a flashlight bulb. After showing me how to hold them together to complete the circuit and light the bulb, I was hooked for life.

I am also indebted to my family for their patience. Particularly my wife Jacqueline, who tries to understand why I need to do the things I do with wires, solder, and parts arriving in the mail. I am glad for even grudging acceptance, because I'm not sure that I could give up the thrill of moving electrons in some new way. Sometimes hobby electronics projects have no real justification beyond "because we can!"

Contents at a Glance

Contents

About the Author

Warren W. Gay started out in electronics at an early age, dragging discarded TVs and radios home from public school. In high school he developed a fascination for programming the IBM 1130 computer, which resulted in a career plan change to software development. After attending Ryerson Polytechnical Institute, he has enjoyed a software developer career for over 30 years, programming mainly in C/C++. Warren has been programming Linux since 1994 as an open source contributor and professionally on various Unix platforms since 1987.

Before attending Ryerson, Warren built an Intel 8008 system from scratch before there were CP/M systems and before computers got personal. In later years, Warren earned an advanced amateur radio license (call sign VE3WWG) and worked the amateur radio satellites. A high point of his ham radio hobby was making digital contact with the Mir space station (U2MIR) in 1991.

Warren works at Datablocks.net, an enterprise-class ad serving software services company. There he programs C++ server solutions on Linux back-end systems.

About the Technical Reviewer

Stewart Watkiss graduated from the University of Hull, United Kingdom, with a masters degree in electronic engineering. He has been a fan of Linux since first installing it on a home computer during the late 1990s. While working as a Linux system administrator, he was awarded Advanced Linux Certification (LPIC 2) in 2006, and created the Penguin Tutor website to help others learning Linux and working toward Linux certification (www.penguintutor.com).

Stewart is a big fan of the Raspberry Pi. He owns several Raspberry Pi computers that he uses to help to protect his home (Internet filter), provide entertainment (XBMC), and teach programming to his two children. He also volunteers as a STEM ambassador, going into local schools to help support teachers and teach programming to teachers and children.

Acknowledgments

In the making of a book, there are so many people involved. I first want to thank Michelle Lowman, acquisitions editor, for her enthusiasm for the initial manuscript and pulling this project together. Enthusiasm goes a long way in an undertaking like this.

I'd also like to thank Kevin Walter, coordinating editor, for handling all my email questions and correspondence, and coordinating things. I greatly appreciated the technical review performed by Stewart Watkiss, checking the facts presented, the formulas, the circuits, and the software. Independent review produces a much better end product.

Thanks also to Sharon Wilkey for patiently wading through the copy edit for me. Judging from the amount of editing, I left her plenty to do. Thanks to Douglas Pundick, development editor, for his oversight and believing in this book. Finally, my thanks to all the other unseen people at Apress who worked behind the scenes to bring this text to print.

I would be remiss if I didn't thank my friends for helping with the initial manuscript. My guitar teacher, Mark Steiger, and my brother-in-law's brother, Erwin Bendiks, both volunteered their time to help me with the first manuscript. Mark has no programming or electronics background and probably deserves an award for reading through "all that stuff." I am indebted also to my daughter Laura and her husband Michael Burton, for taking the time to take my photograph, while planning their wedding at that time.

There are so many others I could list who helped me along the way. To all of you, please accept my humble thanks, and may God bless.

Introduction

The Raspberry Pi, implemented as a System on a Chip (SoC), really does embody the very idea of a "system". There are several large hardware components that make up this complex whole, that we call a system. When we then examine the software side that drives this hardware, we see another body of components that make up the operating system software.

As different as hardware is from software, they form a symbiotic relationship. The hardware provides for external interactions with the world while the software internalizes its inputs and determines the external actions that should result.

Content of this Book

This particular book is focused on system software aspects of the Raspberry Pi. The content was extracted from the complete volume "Mastering the Raspberry Pi" for those that want to focus on this area alone.

While the Pi is not restricted to running one operating system, this title assumes that the student will be working with Raspbian Linux. This is the platform supported by the Raspberry Pi Foundation and as a result, will represent the easiest path for learning.

Chapter 1 covers some very basic things that the beginning student may want to hit the ground running with. Things like setting up a static IP address, using ssh and VNC. Chapter two then jumps right into what happens when your Raspberry Pi boots. Files connected with booting and boot configuration is covered as a reference. But what happens after booting? Chapter 3 looks at how Raspbian Linux pulls itself up from its bootstraps. It examines how services get started and terminated.

Chapter 4 documents the vcgencmd command, which is unique to the Raspberry Pi. It reports and configures special aspects of the hardware. The Linux Console chapter covers the configuration of Linux consoles, including serial port consoles.

Chapters 6 and 7 are important to software developers of the Pi. The first is dedicated to the building and installing a cross-compiler environment for faster, more convenient development on fast hardware like your desktop system. For those that want to modify their Linux kernel, the last chapter is for you. This chapter will guide you through the steps needed to customize and build the Raspbian Linux kernel.

Assumptions about the Reader

Linux tends to be used as a catchall name to include more than just the kernel. In fact some people suggest that it should be referred to as GNU/Linux instead. This is because so much of the involved software is actually provided by the Free Software Foundation

(FSF), aside from the Linux kernel. However you wish to frame it, the reader is assumed to either have some experience with Linux, or is developing some along the way.

For the section about Raspbian Linux initialization, knowledge of shell programming is an asset when creating or modifying the system startup procedures. Otherwise, a basic concept of Linux processes is sufficient for understanding.

Users of cross-compilers for application software development are expected to have some familiarity with the Linux developer tools. This includes the make command and the compiler/linker. Building the kernel can be done by the less experienced, but developer experience is an asset.

Working with the Raspberry Pi often results in bumping into a number of terms and acronyms like GPU or TCP. This book has assumed an intermediate to advanced level audience and consequently these terms are generally not explained. For readers encountering these terms for the first time, the Glossary in Appendix A is there to help.

Finally, as the end user installs or configures his Raspberry Pi, some of the example administration commands found in Appendix C may be useful as a cheat sheet. In most cases, the commands necessary will have already been presented in the text where needed. Mac OS X users will also find Mac specific tips in Appendix E.

CHAPTER 1

Preparation

While it is assumed that you've already started with the Raspberry Pi, there may be a few things that you want to do before working through the rest of this book. For example, if you normally use a laptop or desktop computer, you may prefer to access your Pi from there. Consequently, some of the preparation in this chapter pertains to network access.

If you plan to do most or all of the projects in this book, I highly recommend using something like the Adafruit Pi Cobbler (covered later in this chapter). This hardware breaks out the GPIO lines in a way that you can access them on a breadboard. If you're industrious, you could build a prototyping station out of a block of wood. I took this approach but would buy the Adafruit Pi Cobbler if I were to do it again (this was tedious work).

Static IP Address

The standard Raspbian SD card image provides a capable Linux system, which when plugged into a network, uses DHCP to automatically assign an IP address to it. If you'd like to connect to it remotely from a desktop or laptop, then the dynamic IP address that DHCP assigns is problematic.

There are downloadable Windows programs for scanning the network. If you are using a Linux or Mac host, you can use Nmap to scan for it. The following is an example session from a MacBook Pro, using the MacPorts collection nmap command. Here a range of IP addresses are scanned from 1–254:

```
$ sudo nmap -sP 192.168.0.1-254
Starting Nmap 6.25 (http://nmap.org) at 2013-04-14 19:12 EDT
. . .
Nmap scan report for mac (192.168.0.129)
Host is up.
Nmap scan report for rasp (192.168.0.132)
Host is up (0.00071s latency).
MAC Address : B8:27:EB:2B:69:E8 (Raspberry Pi Foundation)
Nmap done : 254 IP addresses (6 hosts up) scanned in 6.01 seconds
$
```

In this example, the Raspberry Pi is clearly identified on 192.168.0.132, complete with its MAC address. While this discovery approach works, it takes time and is inconvenient.

If you'd prefer to change your Raspberry Pi to use a static IP address, you can find instructions in the "Wired Ethernet" section in Chapter 7 of *Raspberry Pi Hardware Reference* (Apress, 2014).

Using SSH

If you know the IP address of your Raspberry Pi or have the name registered in your hosts file, you can log into it by using SSH. In this example, we log in as user pi on a host named rasp (in this example, from a Mac):

```
$ ssh pi@rasp
pi@rasp's password:
Linux raspberrypi 3.2.27+ #250 PREEMPT ... armv6l
...
Last login : Fri Jan 18 22:19:50 2013 from 192.168.0.179
$
```

Files can also be copied to and from the Raspberry Pi, using the scp command. Do a man scp on the Raspberry Pi to find out more.

It is possible to display X Window System (X-Window) graphics on your laptop/ desktop, if there is an X-Window server running on it. (Windows users can use Cygwin for this, available from www.cygwin.com.) Using Apple's OS X as an example, first configure the security of your X-Window server to allow requests. Here I'll take the lazy approach of allowing all hosts (performed on the Mac) by using the xhost command:

```
$ xhost +
access control disabled, clients can connect from any host
$
```

From the Raspberry Pi, connected through the SSH session, we can launch Xpdf, so that it opens a window on the Mac:

```
$ export DISPLAY=192.168.0.179:0
$ xpdf &
```

Here, I've specified the Mac's IP address (alternatively, an /etc/hosts name could be used) and pointed the Raspberry Pi to use the Mac's display number :0. Then we run the xpdf command in the background, so that we can continue to issue commands in the current SSH session. In the meantime, the Xpdf window will open on the Mac, while the Xpdf program runs on the Raspberry Pi.

This doesn't give you graphical access to the Pi's desktop, but for developers, SSH is often adequate. If you want remote graphical access to the Raspberry's desktop, see the next section, where VNC is introduced.

VNC

If you're already using a laptop or your favorite desktop computer, you can conveniently access your Raspberry Pi's graphical desktop over the network. Once the Raspberry Pi's VNC server is installed, all you need is a VNC client on your accessing computer. Once this is available, you no longer need a keyboard, mouse, or HDMI display device connected to the Raspberry Pi. Simply power up the Pi on your workbench, with a network cable plugged into it.

You can easily install the VNC server software on the Pi at the cost of about 10.4 MB in the root file system. The command to initiate the download and installation is as follows:

```
$ sudo apt-get install tightvncserver
```

After the software is installed, the only remaining step is to configure your access to the desktop. The vncserver command starts up a server, after which you can connect remotely to it.

Using SSH to log in on the Raspberry Pi, type the following command:

```
$ vncserver :1 –geometry 1024x740 –depth 16 –pixelformat rgb565
```

You will require a password to access your desktop.

```
Password:
Verify:
Would you like to enter a view-only password (y/n ) ? n
New 'X' desktop is rasp:1

Creating default startup script/home/pi/.vnc/xstartup Starting applications
specified in/home/pi/.vnc/xstartup
Log file is/home/pi/.vnc/rasp:1.log
$
```

The password prompts are presented only the first time that you start the VNC server.

Display Number

In the vncserver command just shown, the first argument identifies the display number. Your normal Raspberry Pi X-Window desktop is on display :0. So when you start up a VNC server, choose a new unique display number like :1. It doesn't have to be the number 1. To a limited degree, you can run multiple VNC servers if you find that useful. For example, you might choose to start another VNC server on :2 with a different display resolution.

Geometry

The -geometry 1024x740 argument configures the VNC server's resolution in pixels. This example's resolution is unusual in that normally 1024×768 would be used for a display resolution, a common geometry choice for monitors. But this need not be tied to a *physical* monitor resolution. I chose the unusual height of ×740 to prevent the VNC client program from using scrollbars (on a Mac). Some experimentation may be required to find the best geometry to use.

Depth

The -depth 16 argument is the pixel-depth specification. Higher depths are possible, but the resulting additional network trafficc might curb your enthusiasm.

Pixel Format

The last command-line argument given is -pixelformat rgb565. This particular example specifies that each pixel is 5 bits, 6 bits, 5 bits—for red, green and blue, respectively.

Password Setup

To keep unauthorized people from accessing your VNC server, a password is accepted from you when you start the server for the first time. The password chosen can be changed later with the vncpasswd command.

Server Startup

If you often use VNC, you may want to define a personal script or alias to start it on demand. Alternatively, have it started automatically by the Raspberry Pi as part of the Linux initialization. See Chapter 3 for more information about initialization scripts.

VNC Viewers

To access your VNC server on the Raspberry Pi, you need a corresponding VNC viewer on the client side. On the Mac, you can use the MacPorts collection to install a viewer:

```
$ sudo port install vnc
```

Once the viewer is installed, you can access your VNC server on the Raspberry Pi at 192.168.0.170, display :1, with this:

```
$ vncviewer 192.168.0.170:1
```

If you have your Raspberry Pi in the hosts file under rasp, you can use the name instead:

```
$ vncviewer rasp:1
```

When the VNC viewer connects to the server, you will be prompted for a password. This obviously keeps others out of your VNC server.

For Ubuntu Linux, you can install the xvnc4viewer package. For Windows, several choices are available, such as RealVNC and TightVNC.

If you find that the screen resolution doesn't work well with your client computer, experiment with different VNC server resolutions (-geometry). I prefer to use a resolution that doesn't result in scrollbars in the viewer. Scrolling around your Raspberry Pi desktop is a nuisance. You can eliminate the need for scrolling by reducing the geometry dimensions.

Stopping VNC Server

Normally, you don't need to stop the VNC server if you are just going to reboot or shut down your Raspberry Pi. But if you want to stop the VNC server without rebooting, this can be accomplished. Supply the display number that you used in the VNC server startup (:1 in this example) using the -kill option:

```
$ vncserver -kill :1
```

This can be useful as a security measure, or to save CPU resources when the server isn't being used. This can also be useful if you suspect a VNC software problem and need to restart it.

Prototype Station

The danger of working with the tiny Raspberry Pi's PCB is that it moves all over the surface as wires tug at it. Given its low mass, it moves easily and can fall on the floor and short wires out in the process (especially around curious cats).

For this reason, I mounted my Raspberry Pi on a nice block of wood. A small plank can be purchased from the lumberyard for a modest amount. I chose to use teak since it looks nice and doesn't crack or warp. Even if you choose to use something like the Adafruit Pi Cobbler, you may find it useful to anchor the Raspberry Pi PCB. Mount the PCB on the wood with spacers. Figure 1-1 shows my prototype station.

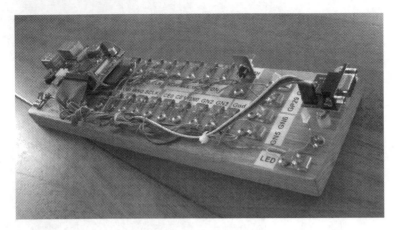

Figure 1-1. *A simple prototype station*

Retro Fahnestock clips were installed and carefully wired to a connector on header strip P1 (the wiring was the most labor-intensive part of this project).

■ **Tip**   Fahnestock clips can be economically purchased at places like www.tubesandmore.com (part # S-H11-4043-6).

A small PCB for the RS-232 interface was acquired from eBay ($2.32 total) and mounted at the end of the station. Wires from the RS-232 PCB were routed back to RX/TX and +3.3 V clips and simply clipped into place (this allows you to disconnect them, if you wish to use those GPIO pins for some other purpose). The RS-232 PCB is permanently grounded for convenience.

The RS-232 PCB is necessary only for those who wish to use a serial console or to interface with some other serial device. The PCB acquired was advertised on eBay as "MAX232CSE Transfer Chip RS-232 To TTL Converter Module COM Serial Board." The converter (based on the MAX232CSE chip) will work with TTL or 3.3 V interfaces. Connecting the RS-232 converter's VCC connection to the Raspberry Pi +3.3 V supply makes it compatible with the Pi.

■ **Caution**   Do not connect the RS-232 converter to +5 V, or you will damage the Pi. For additional information about this, see Chapter 9 of *Raspberry Pi Hardware Reference* (Apress, 2014).

In Figure 1-1 you can see a simple bracket holding a small push button (top right). This has been wired up to P6 for a reset button. This is not strictly required if your power supply is working correctly (power-on reset works rather well). Unlike an AVR setup, *you are not likely to use reset very often.* Chapter 3 of *Raspberry Pi Hardware Reference* (Apress, 2014) has more details about this.

The LED was added to the station last. It was soldered to a pair of half-inch finishing nails, nailed into the wood. The LED's cathode has a 220 Ω resister soldered in series with it to limit the current and wired to ground. The anode is connected to the Fahnestock clip labeled LED. The LED can be tested by connecting an alligator lead from the LED clip to the +3.3 V supply clip (this LED also tolerates +5 V). Be sure to choose a low- to medium-current LED that requires about 10 mA or less (16 mA is the maximum source current from a GPIO pin).

To test your prototyping station, you may want to use the script listed in the "GPIO Tester" section in Chapter 10 of *Raspberry Pi Hardware Reference* (Apress, 2014). That script can be used to blink a given GPIO pin on and off in 1-second intervals.

Adafruit Pi Cobbler

A much easier approach to prototype connections for GPIO is to simply purchase the Adafruit Pi Cobbler kit, which is available from the following site:

```
learn.adafruit.com/adafruit-pi-cobbler-kit/overview
```

This kit provides you with these features:

- Header connector for the Pi's P1
- Ribbon cable
- Small breakout PCB
- Breakout header pins

After assembly, you plug the ribbon cable onto the header P1. At the other end of the ribbon cable is a small PCB that provides 26 pins that plug into your prototype breadboard. A small amount of assembly is required.

Gertboard

Students might consider using a Gertboard, which is available from this site:

```
uk.farnell.com
```

The main reason behind this recommendation is that the Raspberry Pi's connections to the outside world are sensitive, 3.3 V, and vulnerable to static electricity. Students will want to connect all manner of buttons, switches, motors, and relays. Many of these interfaces require additional buffers and drivers, which is what the Gertboard is there for.

In addition to providing the usual access to the Pi's GPIO pins, the Gertboard also provides these features:

- Twelve *buffered* I/O pins

- Three push buttons

- Six open collector drivers (up to 50 V, 500 mA)

- A motor controller (18 V, 2 A)

- A two-channel 8/10/12 bit digital-to-analog converter

- A two-channel 10-bit analog-to-digital converter

- A 28-pin DIP ATmega microcontroller

This provides a ready-made learning environment for the student, who is anxious to wire up something and just "make it work." Many of the 3-volt logic and buffering concerns are eliminated, allowing the student to focus on projects.

Bare Metal

Despite the availability of nice adapters like the Gertboard, the focus of this text is on interfacing directly to the Pi's 3 V GPIO pins. Here are some of the reasons:

- No specific adapter has to be purchased for the projects in this book.

- Any specified adapter can go out of production.

- You'll not likely use an expensive adapter on each *deployed* Pi.

- Bare metal interfacing will exercise your design skills.

If we were to do projects with only wiring involved, there wouldn't be much learning involved. Facing the design issues that arise from working with weak 3 V GPIOs driving the outside world will be much more educational.

The third bullet speaks to finished projects. If you're building a robot, for example, you're not going to buy Gertboards everywhere you need to control a motor or read sensor data. You're going to want to economize and build that yourself. This book is designed to help you *face* those kinds of challenges.

CHAPTER 2

Boot

When the power is first applied to the Raspberry Pi, or it has been reset (for more information, see the "Reset" section in Chapter 3 of *Raspberry Pi Hardware Reference* [Apress, 2014]), a *boot sequence* is initiated. As you will see in this chapter, it is the GPU that actually brings up the ARM CPU.

The way that the Raspberry Pi is designed, it *must* be booted from firmware found on the SD card. It cannot boot from any other source. RISC code for the GPU is provided by the Raspberry Pi Foundation in the file bootcode.bin.

After the second-stage boot loader has been executed, it is possible that other operating systems or ARM boot loaders such as U-Boot can be initiated.

Booting ARM Linux

Generally speaking, Linux under the ARM architecture needs a small amount of assistance to get started. The following are some of the minimal things that the boot loader needs to do:[25]

1. Initialize and configure memory (with MMU, cache, and DMA disabled)

2. Load the kernel image into memory

3. Optionally, load an initial RAM disk image

4. Initialize and provide boot parameters to the loaded kernel (ATAG list)

5. Obtain/determine the Linux machine type (MACH_TYPE)

6. Execute the kernel image with the correct starting register values (r1 = machine number, r2 points to the ATAG list)

7. Additionally, the boot loader is expected to perform some initialization of a serial and/or video console.

In the Raspberry Pi, this boot-loading assistance comes from the embedded GPU in the SoC. The GPU supports a small RISC core that is able to run from initial code found in its ROM. From this small amount of code, the GPU is able to initialize itself and the SD card hardware. From the media on the SD card, it is able to bootstrap itself the rest of the way. For this reason, the Raspberry Pi must always bootstrap from an SD card.

9

Boot Sequence

This section looks at the startup sequence in greater detail. The participating hardware components, the files and data elements are considered. The boot procedure consists of the following sequence of events:

1. At power-up (or reset), the ARM CPU is offline.[23]

2. A small RISC core in the GPU begins to execute SoC ROM code (first-stage boot loader).

3. The GPU initializes the SD card hardware.

4. The GPU looks at the first FAT32 partition in the SD media. (There remains some question about specific limitations as Broadcom has documented this—for example, can it boot from a first FAT16 partition?)

5. The second-stage boot-loader firmware named bootcode.bin is loaded into the GPU.

6. The GPU control passes to the loaded bootcode.bin firmware (SDRAM is initially disabled).

7. The file start.elf is loaded by the GPU into RAM from the SD card.

8. An additional file, fixup.dat, is used to configure the SDRAM partition between GPU and ARM CPU.

9. The file config.txt is examined for configuration parameters that need to be processed.

10. Information found in cmdline.txt is presumably also passed to start.elf.

11. The GPU allows the ARM CPU to execute the program start.elf.

12. The module start.elf runs on the ARM CPU, with information about the kernel to be loaded.

13. The kernel is loaded, and execution control passes to it.

Boot Files

The FAT32 partition containing the boot files is normally mounted as /boot, after Raspbian Linux has come up. Table 2-1 lists the files that apply to the boot process. The text files can be edited to affect new configurations. The binary files can also be replaced by new revisions of the same.

Table 2-1. */boot Files*

File Name	Purpose	Format
bootcode.bin	Second-stage boot loader	Binary
fixup.dat	Configure split of GPU/CPU SDRAM	Binary
config.txt	Configuration parameters	Text
cmdline.txt	Command-line parameters for kernel	Text
start.elf	ARM CPU code to be launched	Binary
kernel.img	Kernel to be loaded	Binary
	Name can be overridden with kernel= parameter in config.txt	

config.txt

The config.txt file permits you to configure many aspects of the boot process. Some options affect physical devices, and others affect the kernel being loaded.

Composite Video Settings

The composite video output from the Raspberry Pi is primarily configured by three basic parameters:

- sdtv_mode
- sdtv_aspect
- sdtv_disable_colourburst

Standard Definition Video

The parameter sdtv_mode determines the video mode (TV standard) of the composite video output jack.

sdtv_mode	Description
0	Normal NTSC (default)
1	Japanese NTSC (no pedestal)
2	Normal PAL
3	Brazilian PAL 525/60

Composite Aspect Ratio

The sdtv_aspect parameter configures the composite video aspect ratio.

sdtv_aspect	Description
1	4:3 (default)
2	14:9
3	16:9

Color Burst

By default, color burst is enabled. This permits the generation of color out of the composite video jack. Setting the video for monochrome may be desirable for a sharper display.

sdtv_disable_colourburst	Description
0	Color burst enabled (default)
1	Color burst disabled (monochrome)

High-Definition Video

This section covers config.txt settings that affect HDMI operation.

HDMI Safe Mode

The hdmi_safe parameter enables support of automatic HDMI configuration for optimal compatibility.

hdmi_safe	Description
0	Disabled (default)
1	Enabled

When hdmi_safe=1 (enabled), the following settings are implied:

- hdmi_force_hotplug=1
- config_hdmi_boost=4
- hdmi_group=1
- hdmi_mode=1
- disable_overscan=0

HDMI Force Hot-Plug

This configuration setting allows you to force a hot-plug signal for the HDMI display, whether the display is connected or not. The NOOBS distribution enables this setting by default.

hdmi_force_hotplug	Description
0	Disabled (non-NOOBS default)
1	Use HDMI mode even when no HDMI monitor is detected (NOOBS default)

HDMI Ignore Hot-Plug

Enabling the hdmi_ignore_hotplug setting causes it to appear to the system that no HDMI display is attached, even if there is. This can help force composite video output, while the HDMI display is plugged in.

hdmi_ignore_hotplug	Description
0	Disabled (default)
1	Use composite video even if an HDMI display is detected

HDMI Drive

This mode allows you to choose between DVI (no sound) and HDMI mode (with sound, when supported).

hdmi_drive	Description
1	Normal DVI mode (no sound)
2	Normal HDMI mode (sound will be sent if supported and enabled)

13

HDMI Ignore EDID

Enabling this option causes the EDID information from the display to be ignored. Normally, this information is helpful and is used.

hdmi_ignore_edid	Description
Unspecified	Read EDID information
0xa5000080	Ignore EDID information

HDMI EDID File

When hdmi_edid_file is enabled, the EDID information is taken from the file named edid.txt. Otherwise, it is taken from the display, when available.

hdmi_edid_file	Description
0	Read EDID data from device (default)
1	Read EDID data from edid.txt file

HDMI Force EDID Audio

Enabling this option forces the support of all audio formats even if the display does not support them. This permits pass-through of DTS/AC3 when reported as unsupported.

hdmi_force_edid_audio	Description
0	Use EDID-provided values (default)
1	Pretend all audio formats are supported

Avoid EDID Fuzzy Match

Avoid fuzzy matching of modes described in the EDID.

avoid_edid_fuzzy_match	Description
0	Use fuzzy matching (default)
1	Avoid fuzzy matching

HDMI Group

The hdmi_group option defines the HDMI type.

hdmi_group	Description
0	Use the preferred group reported by the EDID (default)
1	CEA
2	DMT

HDMI Mode

This option defines the screen resolution to use in CEA or DMT format (see the parameter hdmi_group in the preceding subsection "HDMI Group"). In Table 2-2, the modifiers shown have the following meanings:

    H means 16:9 variant of a normally 4:3 mode.

    2x means pixel doubled (higher clock rate).

    4x means pixel quadrupled (higher clock rate).

    R means reduced blanking (fewer bytes are used for blanking within the data stream, resulting in lower clock rates).

Table 2-2. *HDMI Mode Settings*

Group Mode	CEA Resolution	Refresh	Modifiers	DMT Resolution	Refresh	Notes
1	VGA			640×350	85 Hz	
2	480 p	60 Hz		640×400	85 Hz	
3	480 p	60 Hz	H	720×400	85 Hz	
4	720 p	60 Hz		640×480	60 Hz	
5	1080 i	60 Hz		640×480	72 Hz	
6	480 i	60 Hz		640×480	75 Hz	
7	480 i	60 Hz	H	640×480	85 Hz	
8	240 p	60 Hz		800×600	56 Hz	
9	240 p	60 Hz	H	800×600	60 Hz	
10	480 i	60 Hz	4x	800×600	72 Hz	

(continued)

Table 2-2. *(continued)*

Group Mode	CEA Resolution	Refresh	Modifiers	DMT Resolution	Refresh	Notes
11	480 i	60 Hz	4x H	800×600	75 Hz	
12	240 p	60 Hz	4x	800×600	85 Hz	
13	240 p	60 Hz	4x H	800×600	120 Hz	
14	480 p	60 Hz	2x	848×480	60 Hz	
15	480 p	60 Hz	2x H	1024×768	43 Hz	Don't use
16	1080 p	60 Hz		1024×768	60 Hz	
17	576 p	50 Hz		1024×768	70 Hz	
18	576 p	50 Hz	H	1024×768	75 Hz	
19	720 p	50 Hz		1024×768	85 Hz	
20	1080 i	50 Hz		1024×768	120 Hz	
21	576 i	50 Hz		1152×864	75 Hz	
22	576 i	50 Hz	H	1280×768		R
23	288 p	50 Hz		1280×768	60 Hz	
24	288 p	50 Hz	H	1280×768	75 Hz	
25	576 i	50 Hz	4x	1280×768	85 Hz	
26	576 i	50 Hz	4x H	1280×768	120 Hz	R
27	288 p	50 Hz	4x	1280×800		R
28	288 p	50 Hz	4x H	1280×800	60 Hz	
29	576 p	50 Hz	2x	1280×800	75 Hz	
30	576 p	50 Hz	2x H	1280×800	85 Hz	
31	1080 p	50 Hz		1280×800	120 Hz	R
32	1080 p	24 Hz		1280×960	60 Hz	
33	1080 p	25 Hz		1280×960	85 Hz	
34	1080 p	30 Hz		1280×960	120 Hz	R
35	480 p	60 Hz	4x	1280×1024	60 Hz	
36	480 p	60 Hz	4x H	1280×1024	75 Hz	

(continued)

Table 2-2. *(continued)*

Group Mode	CEA Resolution	Refresh	Modifiers	DMT Resolution	Refresh	Notes
37	576 p	50 Hz	4x	1280×1024	85 Hz	
38	576 p	50 Hz	4x H	1280×1024	120 Hz	R
39	1080 i	50 Hz	R	1360×768	60 Hz	
40	1080 i	100 Hz		1360×768	120 Hz	R
41	720 p	100 Hz		1400×1050		R
42	576 p	100 Hz		1400×1050	60 Hz	
43	576 p	100 Hz	H	1400×1050	75 Hz	
44	576 i	100 Hz		1400×1050	85 Hz	
45	576 i	100 Hz	H	1400×1050	120 Hz	R
46	1080 i	120 Hz		1440×900		R
47	720 p	120 Hz		1440×900	60 Hz	
48	480 p	120 Hz		1440×900	75 Hz	
49	480 p	120 Hz	H	1440×900	85 Hz	
50	480 i	120 Hz		1440×900	120 Hz	R
51	480 i	120 Hz	H	1600×1200	60 Hz	
52	576 p	200 Hz		1600×1200	65 Hz	
53	576 p	200 Hz	H	1600×1200	70 Hz	
54	576 i	200 Hz		1600×1200	75 Hz	
55	576 i	200 Hz	H	1600×1200	85 Hz	
56	480 p	240 Hz		1600×1200	120 Hz	R
57	480 p	240 Hz	H	1680×1050		R
58	480 i	240 Hz		1680×1050	60 Hz	
59	480 i	240 Hz	H	1680×1050	75 Hz	
60				1680×1050	85 Hz	
61				1680×1050	120 Hz	R
62				1792×1344	60 Hz	
63				1792×1344	75 Hz	

(continued)

17

Table 2-2. *(continued)*

Group	CEA			DMT		
Mode	Resolution	Refresh	Modifiers	Resolution	Refresh	Notes
64				1792×1344	120 Hz	R
65				1856×1392	60 Hz	
66				1856×1392	75 Hz	
67				1856×1392	120 Hz	R
68				1920×1200		R
69				1920×1200	60 Hz	
70				1920×1200	75 Hz	
71				1920×1200	85 Hz	
72				1920×1200	120 Hz	R
73				1920×1440	60 Hz	
74				1920×1440	75 Hz	
75				1920×1440	120 Hz	R
76				2560×1600		R
77				2560×1600	60 Hz	
78				2560×1600	75 Hz	
79				2560×1600	85 Hz	
80				2560×1600	120 Hz	R
81				1366×768	60 Hz	
82	1080 p	60 Hz				
83				1600×900		R
84				2048×1152		R
85	720 p	60 Hz				
86				1366×768		R

HDMI Boost

The config_hdmi_boost parameter allows you to tweak the HDMI signal strength.

config_hdmi_boost	Description
0	Non-NOOBS default
1	
2	
3	
4	Use if you have interference issues (NOOBS default setting)
5	
6	
7	Maximum strength

HDMI Ignore CEC Init

When this option is enabled, the CEC initialization is not sent to the device. This avoids bringing the TV out of standby and channel switch when rebooting.

hdmi_ignore_cec_init	Description
0	Normal (default)
1	Don't send initial active source message

HDMI Ignore CEC

When this option is enabled, the assumption made is that CEC is not supported at all by the HDMI device, even if the device does have support. As a result, no CEC functions will be supported.

hdmi_ignore_cec	Description
0	Normal (default)
1	Disable CEC support

Overscan Video

A few options control the overscan support of the composite video output. When overscan is enabled, a certain number of pixels are skipped at the sides of the screen as configured.

Disable Overscan

The `disable_overscan` option can disable the overscan feature. It is enabled by default:

disable_overscan	Description
0	Overscan enabled (default)
1	Overscan disabled

Overscan Left, Right, Top, and Bottom

These parameters control the number of pixels to skip at the left, right, top, and bottom of the screen.

Parameter	Pixels to Skip
overscan_left=0	At left
overscan_right=0	At right
overscan_top=0	At top
overscan_bottom=0	At bottom

Frame Buffer Settings

The Linux frame buffer support is configured by a few configuration options described in this section.

Frame Buffer Width

The default is to define the width of the frame buffer as the display's width minus the overscan pixels.

framebuffer_width	Description
default	Display width overscan
framebuffer_width=n	Set width to n pixels

Frame Buffer Height

The default is to define the height of the frame buffer as the display's height minus the overscan pixels.

framebuffer_height	Description
default	Display height overscan
framebuffer_height=n	Set height to *n* pixels

Frame Buffer Depth

This parameter defines the number of bits per pixel.

framebuffer_depth	Description
8	Valid, but default RGB palette makes an unreadable screen
16	Default
24	Looks better but has corruption issues as of 6/15/2012
32	No corruption, but requires framebuffer_ignore_alpha=1, and shows wrong colors as of 6/15/2012

Frame Buffer Ignore Alpha

The alpha channel can be disabled with this option. As of this writing, this option must be used when using a frame buffer depth of 32 bits.

framebuffer_ignore_alpha	Description
0	Alpha channel enabled (default)
1	Alpha channel disabled

General Video Options

The display can be flipped or rotated in different ways, according to the display_rotate option. You should be able to do both a flip and a rotate by adding the flip values to the rotate value.

■ **Note**   I was unable to get the flip options to work on Linux Raspberry Pi 3.2.27+ #250. It is possible that a newer version of the boot-loader `bootcode.bin` may be needed. But as of 2014, this remains an issue.

The 90° and 270° rotations require additional memory on the GPU, so these options won't work with a 16 MB GPU split.

display_rotate	Description
0	0° (default)
1	90°
2	180°
3	270°
0x1000	Horizontal flip
0x2000	Vertical flip

While the flip options are documented, I was unable to get them to work. The rotations, however, were confirmed as working.

Licensed Codecs

The following options permit you to configure the purchased license key codes for the codecs they affect.

Option	Notes
decode_MPG2=0x12345678	License key for hardware MPEG-2 decoding
decode_WVC1=0x12345678	License key for hardware VC-1 decoding

Testing

The following test option enables image/sound tests during boot. This is intended for manufacturer testing.

test_mode	Description
0	Disable test mode (default)
1	Enable test mode

Memory

This section summarizes configuration settings pertaining to memory.

Disable GPU L2 Cache

The disable_l2cache option allows the ARM CPU access to the GPU L2 cache to be disabled. This needs the corresponding L2 disabled in the kernel.

disable_l2cache	Description
0	Enable GPU L2 cache access (default)
1	Disable GPU L2 cache access

GPU Memory (All)

The gpu_mem option allows configuration of the GPU memory for all Raspberry Pi board revisions (unless gpu_mem_256 or gpu_mem_512 is supplied).

gpu_mem	Description
gpu_mem=64	Default is 64 MB
gpu_mem=128	128 MB

GPU Memory (256)

The gpu_mem_256 option allows configuration of the GPU memory for the 256 MB Raspberry Pi boards. When specified, it overrides the gpu_mem option setting.

gpu_mem_256	Description
unspecified	Defined by gpu_mem option
gpu_mem_256=128	128 MB (example)

GPU Memory (512)

The gpu_mem_512 option configures the GPU memory allocated for the 512 MB Raspberry Pi boards. When specified, it overrides the gpu_mem option setting.

gpu_mem_512	Description
unspecified	Defined by gpu_mem option
gpu_mem_512=128	128 MB (example)

Boot Options

Several options in this section affect the boot process. Many options pertain to the kernel being started, while others affect file systems and devices.

Disable Command-Line Tags

The disable_commandline_tags option permits the user to prevent start.elf from filling in ATAGS memory before launching the kernel. This prevents the cmdline.txt file from being supplied to the kernel at boot time.

disable_commandline_tags	Description
0	Enable ATAGS (default)
1	Disable command line in ATAGS

Command Line

The cmdline option allows you to configure the kernel command-line parameters within the config.txt file, instead of the cmdline.txt file.

cmdline	Description
unspecified	Command line is taken from cmdline.txt
cmdline="command"	Command line is taken from parameter

Kernel

By default, start.elf loads the kernel from the file named kernel.img. Specifying the kernel parameter allows the user to change the file's name.

kernel	Description
unspecified	kernel="kernel.img" (default)
kernel="plan9.img"	kernel="plan9.img"

Kernel Address

This parameter determines the memory address where the kernel image is loaded into.

kernel_address	Description
0x00000000	Default

RAM File System File

The ramfsfile parameter names the file for the RAM FS file, to be used with the kernel.

ramfsfile	Description
unspecified	No RAM FS file used
ramfsfile="ramfs.file"	File ramfs.file is used

RAM File System Address

The ramfsaddr parameter specifies where the RAM file system image is to be loaded into memory.

ramfsaddr	Description
0x00000000	Default address

Init RAM File System

This option is a convenience option, which combines the options `ramfsfile` and `ramfsaddr`.

initramfs	Arg 1	Arg 2	Description
initramfs	initram.gz	0x00800000	Example

Device Tree Address

The `device_tree_address` option defines where the device tree address is loaded.

device_tree_address	Description
0x00000000	Default

Init UART Baud

The `init_uart_baud` option allows the user to reconfigure the serial console to use a baud rate that is different from the default.

init_uart_baud	Description
115200	Default baud rate

Init UART Clock

The `init_uart_clock` parameter permits the user to reconfigure the UART to use a different clock rate.

init_uart_clock	Description
3000000	Default

Init EMMC Clock

The `init_emmc_clock` parameter allows the user to tweak the EMMC clock, which can improve the SD card performance.

init_emmc_clock	Description
100000000	Default

Boot Delay

The boot_delay and boot_delay_ms options allow the user to reconfigure the delay used by start.elf prior to loading the kernel. The actual delay time used is computed from the following:

$$D = 1000 \times b + m$$

where

- D is the computed delay in milliseconds.
- b is the boot_delay value.
- m is the boot_delay_ms value.

boot_delay (b)	Description
1	Default

The boot_delay_ms augments the boot_delay parameter.

boot_delay_ms (m)	Description
0	Default

Avoid Safe Mode

A jumper or switch can be placed between pins P1-05 (GPIO 1) and P1-06 (ground) to cause start.elf to initiate a *safe mode* boot. If GPIO 1 is being used for some other I/O function, the safe mode check should be disabled.

avoid_safe_mode	Description
0	Default (check P1-05 for safe mode)
1	Disable safe mode check

Overclocking

According to the Raspberry Pi Configuration Settings file, Revision 14 (http://elinux.org/RPi_config.txt) the ARM CPU, SDRAM, and GPU have their own clock signals (from a PLL). The GPU core, H.264, V3D, and ISP all share the same clock.

The following commands can be used to check your CPU, once you have a command-line prompt. The /proc/cpuinfo pseudo file will give you a BogoMIPS figure:

```
$ cat /proc/cpuinfo
Processor         : ARMv6-compatible processor rev 7 ( v6l )
BogoMIPS          : 697.95
Features          : swp half thumb fastmult vfp edsp java tls
CPU implementer   : 0x41
CPU architecture  : 7
CPU variant       : 0x0
CPU part          : 0xb76
CPU revision      : 7
Hardware          : BCM2708
Revision          : 000f
Serial            : 00000000 f52b69e9
$
```

The vcgencmd can be used to read the ARM CPU clock frequency:

```
$ vcgencmd measure_clock arm
frequency (45)=700074000
$
```

To configure for overclocking, you start with the phase-locked loop (PLL). The PLL frequency is computed as follows:

$$p = floor\left(\frac{2400}{2c}\right)(2c)$$

where

- p is the computed PLL frequency.

- c is the core frequency.

From this, the GPU frequency multiple m is computed from a trial GPU frequency t as follows:

$$m = \frac{p}{t}$$

The value m is then rounded to the nearest *even* integer value, and the *final* GPU frequency g is computed as follows:

$$g = \frac{p}{m}$$

If we take an example where the core frequency c is 500 MHz, then p is determined as follows:

$$p = floor\left(\frac{2400}{2 \times 500}\right) \times (2 \times 500)$$
$$= 2000$$

Further, if we are targeting a GPU frequency of 300 MHz, we compute m:

$$m = \frac{2000}{300} = 6.666$$

The value m is rounded to the nearest *even* integer:

$$m = 6$$

The final GPU frequency becomes

$$g = \frac{p}{m} = \frac{2000}{6} = 333.33$$

The example GPU clock is 333.33 MHz.

Table 2-3 lists the standard clock profiles, as provided by the Raspberry Pi Foundation. Additionally, it is stated that if the SoC reaches `temp_limit`, the overclock settings will be disabled. The value of `temp_limit` is configurable.

Table 2-3. *Standard Clock Profiles*

Profile	ARM CPU	Core	SDRAM	Over Voltage
None	700 MHz	250 MHz	400 MHz	0
Modest	800 MHz	300 MHz	400 MHz	0
Medium	900 MHz	333 MHz	450 MHz	2
High	950 MHz	450 MHz	450 MHz	6
Turbo	1000 MHz	500 MHz	500 MHz	6

Warranty and Overclocking

At one time, overclocking could void your warranty. Also note that Internet forum users have reported SD card corruption when trying out overclocked configurations (though several improvements to SD card handling have been made). Be sure to back up your SD card.

The following combination of parameters may set a permanent bit in your SoC chip and void your warranty. While the Raspberry Pi announcement (www.raspberrypi.org/introducing-turbo-mode-up-to-50-more-performance-for-free/) speaks of overclocking without voiding the warranty, it is subject to some conditions like using the cpufreq driver. The following conditions may put your warranty in jeopardy:

- ver_voltage > 0, and at least one of the following:

- force_turbo = 1

- current_limit_override = 0x5A000020

- temp_limit > 85

Force Turbo Mode

The documentation indicates that force_turbo has no effect if other overclocking options are in effect.

By default, force_turbo is disabled. When disabled, it disables some other configuration options such as h264_freq. However, enabling force_turbo also enables h264_freq, v3d_freq, and isp_freq.

force_turbo	Description
0 (default)	Enables dynamic clocks and voltage for the ARM core, GPU core, and SDRAM. In this mode, settings for h264_freq, v3d_freq, and isp_freq are ignored.
1	Disables dynamic clocks and voltage for the ARM core, GPU core, and SDRAM. Configuration option values h264_freq, v3d_freq, and isp_freq apply when specified.

Initial Turbo

The initial_turbo option is described in config.txt as "enables turbo mode from boot for the given value in seconds (up to 60)." This is somewhat confusing.

What is meant is that turbo mode will be enabled after a delay of a configured number of seconds after boot. By default, if turbo mode is enabled, it is enabled immediately (after examining config.txt).

The initial_turbo option allows the boot process to proceed at normal clock rates until the process has progressed to a certain point. Some people on Internet forums that experience SD card corruption from overclocking will suggest the initial_turbo option as a solution.

initial_turbo	Description
0	No timed turbo mode (default)
60	Maximum number of seconds after boot before enabling turbo mode

Temperature Limit

The temp_limit configuration option allows the user to override the default safety limit. Increasing this value beyond 85ºC voids your warranty.

When the SoC temperature exceeds temp_limit, the clocks and voltages are set to default values for safer operation.

temp_limit	Description
85	Temperature limit in Celsius (default)
> 85	Voids your warranty

ARM CPU Frequency

The parameter arm_freq sets the clock frequency of the ARM CPU in MHz. This option applies in non-turbo and turbo modes.

arm_freq	Description
700	Default ARM CPU frequency, in MHz
> 700	May void warranty—check related conditions

Minimum ARM CPU Frequency

This option can be used when using dynamic clocking of the ARM CPU. This sets the lowest clock speed for the ARM.

arm_freq_min	Description
700	Default ARM CPU frequency in MHz
> 700	May void warranty—check related conditions

GPU Frequency

The gpu_freq option determines the following other values:

Parameter	MHz
core_freq	Core frequency
h264_freq	H.264 frequency
isp_freq	Image sensor pipeline frequency
v3d_freq	3D video block frequency

The gpu_freq parameter has the following default value:

gpu_freq	Description
250	Default GPU frequency (MHz)

Core Frequency

The core_freq option allows the user to configure the GPU processor core clock. This parameter also affects the ARM performance, since it drives the L2 cache.

core_freq	Description
250	Default in MHz

Minimum Core Frequency

When dynamic clocking is used, this sets the minimum GPU processor core clock rate. See also the core_freq option. Like the core_freq option, this parameter affects the ARM performance, since it drives the L2 cache.

core_freq_min	Description
250	Default in MHz

H.264 Frequency

This parameter configures the frequency of the video block hardware. This parameter applies when force_turbo mode is enabled.

h264_freq	Description
250	Default in MHz

ISP Frequency

This parameter configures the image sensor pipeline clock rate and applies when force_turbo mode is enabled.

isp_freq	Description
250	Default in MHz

V3D Frequency

The v3d_freq configures the 3D block frequency in MHz. This parameter applies when force_turbo mode is enabled.

v3d_freq	Description
250	Default in MHz

SDRAM Frequency

The sdram_freq parameter allows the user to configure frequency of the SDRAM.

sdram_freq	Description
400	Default in MHz

Minimum SDRAM Frequency

When dynamic clocks are used, the `sdram_freq_min` allows the user to configure a minimum clock rate in MHz.

sdram_freq_min	Description
400	Default in MHz

Avoid PWM PLL

The `avoid_pwm_pll` configuration parameter allows the user to unlink the `core_freq` from the rest of the GPU. A Pi configuration note states, "analog audio should still work, but from a fractional divider, so lower quality."

avoid_pwm_pll	Description
0	Linked core_freq (default)
1	Unlinked core_freq

Voltage Settings

The configuration parameters in this subsection configure voltages for various parts of the Raspberry Pi.

Current Limit Override

When supplied, the switched-mode power supply current limit protection is disabled. This can be helpful with overclocking if you are encountering reboot failures.

current_limit_override	Description
Unspecified	Default (limit in effect)
0x5A000020	Disables SMPS current limit protection

Over Voltage

The ARM CPU and GPU core voltage can be adjusted through the `over_voltage` option. Use the values shown in Table 2-4.

Table 2-4. *Voltage Parameter Values*

Parameter	Voltage	Notes
-16	0.8 V	
-15	0.825 V	
-14	0.85 V	
-13	0.875 V	
-12	0.9 V	
-11	0.925 V	
-10	0.95 V	
-9	0.975 V	
-8	1.0 V	
-7	1.025 V	
-6	1.05 V	
-5	1.075 V	
-4	1.1 V	
-3	1.125 V	
-2	1.15 V	
-1	1.175 V	
0	1.2 V	Default
1	1.225 V	
2	1.25 V	
3	1.275 V	
4	1.3 V	
5	1.325 V	
6	1.35 V	
7	1.375 V	Requires force_turbo=1
8	1.4 V	Requires force_turbo=1

Over Voltage Minimum

The over_voltage_min option can be used when dynamic clocking is employed, to prevent the voltage dropping below a specified minimum. Use the values from Table 2-4.

Over Voltage SDRAM

The over_voltage_sdram configuration option is a convenient way to set three options at once:

- over_voltage_sdram_c: SDRAM controller voltage

- over_voltage_sdram_i: SDRAM I/O voltage adjust

- over_voltage_sdram_p: SDRAM physical voltage adjust

Raspberry Pi documentation says the over_voltage_sdram option "sets over_voltage_sdram_c, over_voltage_sdram_i, over_voltage_sdram_p together." Use the values shown in Table 2-4.

SDRAM Controller Voltage

Use the over_voltage_sdram_c option to set the voltage for the SDRAM controller. Use the values shown in Table 2-4. See also the over_voltage_sdram option.

SDRAM I/O Voltage

Use the over_voltage_sdram_i option to set the voltage for the SDRAM I/O subsystem. Use the values shown in Table 2-4. See also the over_voltage_sdram option.

SDRAM Physical Voltage

The over_voltage_sdram_p option adjusts the "physical voltage" for the SDRAM subsystem. Use the values shown in Table 2-4. See also the over_voltage_sdram option.

cmdline.txt

The cmdline.txt file is used to supply command-line arguments to the kernel. The Raspbian values supplied in the standard image are broken into multiple lines here for easier reading (note that the NOOBS distribution may show a different device for the root file system):

```
$ cat /boot/cmdline.txt
dwc_otg.lpm_enable=0 \
 console=ttyAMA0,115200 \
 kgdboc=ttyAMA0,115200 \
```

```
console=tty1 \
root=/dev/mmcblk0p2 \
rootfstype=ext4 \
elevator=deadline \
rootwait
$
```

This file is provided as a convenience, since the parameters can be configured in the config.txt file, using the cmdline="text" option. When the config.txt option is provided, it supersedes the cmdline.txt file.

Once the Raspbian Linux kernel comes up, you can review the command-line options used as follows (edited for readability):

```
$ cat /proc/cmdline
dma.dmachans=0x7f35 \
bcm2708_fb.fbwidth=656 \
bcm2708_fb.fbheight=416 \
bcm2708.boardrev=0x+ \
bcm2708.serial=0xf52b69e9 \
smsc95xx.macaddr=B8:27:EB:2B:69:E9 \
sdhci-bcm2708.emmc_clock_freq=100000000 \
vc_mem.mem_base=0x1c000000 \
vc_mem. mem_size=0x20000000 \
dwc_otg.lpm_enable=0 \
console=ttyAMA0,115200 \
kgdboc=ttyAMA0,115200 \
console=tty1 \
root=/dev/mmcblk0p2 \
rootfstype=ext4 \
elevator=deadline \
rootwait
$
```

Additional options can be seen prepended to what was provided in the cmdline.txt file. Options of the format name.option=values are specific to kernel-loadable modules. For example, the parameter bcm2708_fb.fbwidth=656 pertains to the module bcm2708_fb.

There are too many Linux kernel parameters to describe here (entire books have been written on this topic), but some of the most commonly used ones are covered in the following subsections.

Serial console=

The Linux console parameter specifies to Linux what device to use for a console. For the Raspberry Pi, this is normally specified as follows:

```
console=ttyAMA0,115200
```

This references the serial device that is made available after boot-up as /dev/ttyAMA0. The parameter following the device name is the baud rate (115200).

The general form of the serial console option is as follows:

console=ttyDevice,bbbbpnf

The second parameter is the options field:

Zone	Description	Value	Raspbian Notes
bbbb	Baud rate	115200	Can be more than four digits
p	Parity	n	No parity
		o	Odd parity
		e	Even parity
n	Number of bits	7	7 data bits
		8	8 data bits
f	Flow control	r	RTS
		omitted	No RTS

Virtual console=

Linux supports a virtual console, which is also configurable from the console= parameter. Raspbian Linux specifies the following:

console=tty1

This device is available from /dev/tty1, after the kernel boots up. The tty parameters used for this virtual console can be listed (edited here for readability):

```
$ sudo -i
# stty -a </dev/tty1
speed 38400 baud ; rows 26; columns 82; line = 0;
intr = ^C; quit = ^\; erase = ^?; kill = ^U; \
eof = ^D; eol = <undef>; eol2 = <undef>; swtch = <undef>;
start = ^Q; stop = ^S ; susp = ^Z; rprnt = ^R; werase = ^W; \
lnext = ^V; flush = ^O; min = 1; time = 0;
-parenb -parodd cs8 hupcl -cstopb cread -clocal -crtscts
-ignbrk brkint -ignpar -parmrk -inpck -istrip -inlcr \
-igncr icrnl ixon -ixoff -iuclc -ixany imaxbel iutf8
opost -o lcuc -ocrnl onlcr -onocr -onlret -ofill -ofdel \
nl0 cr0 tab0 bs0 vt0 ff0
isig icanon iexten echo echoe echok -echonl -noflsh \
-xcase -tostop -echoprt -echoctl echoke
#
```

kgdboc=

The kgdboc parameter was named after the idea "kgdb over console." This allows you to use a serial console as your primary console as well as use it for kernel debugging. The primary console, however, need not be a serial console for kgdboc to be used.[27]

The Raspbian image supplies this:

```
kgdboc=ttyAMA0,115200
```

This allows kernel debugging to proceed through serial device /dev/ttyAMA0, which is the only serial device supported on the Raspberry Pi.

root=

The Linux kernel needs to know what device holds the root file system. The standard Raspbian image supplies the following:

```
root=/dev/mmcblk0p2
```

This points the kernel to the SD card (mmcblk0), partition 2 (non-NOOBS distribution). See also the rootfstype parameter.

The general form of the root= parameter supports three forms:

- root=MMmm: Boot from major device MM, minor mm (hexadecimal).

- root-/dev/nfs: Boot a NFS disk specified by nfsroot (see also nfs-root= and ip=).

- root=/dev/name: Boot from a device named /dev/name.

rootfstype=

In addition to specifying the device holding the root file system, the Linux kernel sometimes needs to know the file system type. This is configured through the rootfstype parameter. The standard Raspbian image supplies the following:

```
rootfstype=ext4
```

This example indicates that the root file system is the ext4 type.

The Linux kernel can examine the device given in the root parameter to determine the file system type. But there are scenarios where the kernel cannot resolve the type or gets confused. Otherwise, you may want to force a certain file system type. Another situation is when MTD is used for the root file system. For example, when using JFFS2, it must specified.

elevator=

This option selects the I/O scheduler scheme to be used within the kernel. The standard Raspbian image specifies the following:

```
elevator=deadline
```

To find out the I/O scheduler option being used and the other available choices (in your kernel), we can consult the /sys pseudo file system:

```
$ cat /sys/block/mmcblk0/queue/scheduler
noop [deadline] cfq
$
```

The name mmcblk0 is the name of the device that your root file system is on. The output shows in square brackets that the deadline I/O scheduler is being used. The other choices are noop and cfq. These I/O schedulers are as follows:

Name	Description	Notes
noop	No special ordering of requests	
cfq	Completely fair scheduler	Older
deadline	Cyclic scheduler, but requests have deadlines	Newest

The deadline I/O scheduler is the newest implementation, designed for greater efficiency and fairness. The deadline scheduler uses a cyclic elevator, except that it additionally logs a deadline for the request. A cyclic elevator is one where the requests are ordered according to sector numbers and head movement (forward and backward). The deadline scheduler will use the cyclic elevator behavior, but if it looks like the request is about to expire, it is given immediate priority.

rootwait=

This option is used when the device used for the root file system is a device that is started asynchronously with other kernel boot functions. This is usually needed for USB and MMC devices, which may take extra time to initialize. The rootwait option forces the kernel to wait until the root device becomes ready.

Given that the root file system is on the SD card (a MMC device), the Raspbian image uses the following:

```
rootwait
```

nfsroot=

The nfsroot option permits you to define a kernel that boots from an NFS mount (assuming that NFS support is compiled into the kernel). The square brackets show placement of optional values:

```
nfsroot=[server-ip:]root-dir[,nfs-options]
```

Field	Description
server-ip	NFS server IP number (default uses ip=)
root-dir	Root dir on NFS server. If there is a %s present, the IP address will be inserted there.
nfs-options	NFS options like ro, separated by commas

When unspecified, the default of /tftpboot/client_ip_address will be used. This requires that root=/dev/nfs be specified and optionally ip= may be added.

To test whether you have NFS support in your kernel, you can query the /proc file system when the system has booted:

```
$ cat /proc/filesystems
nodev   sysfs
nodev   rootfs
nodev   bdev
nodev   proc
nodev   cgroup
nodev   tmpfs
nodev   devtmpfs
nodev   debugfs
nodev   sockfs
nodev   pipcfs
nodev   anon_inodefs
nodev   rpc_pipefs
nodev   configfs
nodev   devpts
        ext3
        ext2
        ext4
nodev   ramfs
        vfat
        msdos
nodev   nfs
nodev   nfs4
nodev   autofs
nodev   mqueue
```

From this example, we see that both the older NFS (nfs) and the newer NFS4 file systems are supported.

ip=

This option permits the user to configure the IP address of a network device, or to specify how the IP number is assigned. See also the root= and nfsroot= options.

```
ip=client-ip:server-ip:gw-ip:netmask:hostname:device:autoconf
```

Table 2-5 describes the fields within this option. The autoconf *value* can appear by itself, without the intervening colons if required. When ip=off or ip=none is given, no autoconfiguration takes place. The autoconfiguration protocols are listed in Table 2-6.

Table 2-5. *ip= Kernel Parameter*

Field	Description	Default
ip-client	IP address of the client	Autoconfigured
ip-server	IP address of NFS server, required only for NFS root	Autoconfigured
gw-ip	IP address of server if on a separate subnet	Autoconfigured
netmask	Netmask for local IP address	Autoconfigured
hostname	Hostname to provide to DHCP	Client IP address
device	Name of interface to use	When more than one is available, autoconf
autoconf	Autoconfiguration method	Any

Table 2-6. *Autoconfiguration Protocols*

Protocol	Description
off or none	Don't autoconfigure
on or any	Use any protocol available (default)
dhcp	Use DHCP
bootp	Use BOOTP
rarp	Use RARP
both	Use BOOTP or RARP but not DHCP

Emergency Kernel

In the event that your Raspberry Pi does not boot up properly, an emergency kernel is provided in /boot as file kernel_emergency.img. This kernel includes a BusyBox root file system to provide recovery tools. Through use of e2fsck, you'll be able to repair your normal Linux root file system. If necessary, you'll be able to mount that file system and make changes with the BusyBox tools.

To activate the emergency kernel, mount your SD card in a Linux, Mac, or Windows computer. Your computer should see the FAT32 partition, allowing you to rename files and edit configurations. Rename your current kernel.img to something like kernel.bak (you likely want to restore this kernel image later). Then rename kernel_emergency.img as kernel.img.

If you have used special configuration options in config.txt and cmdline.txt, you should copy these to config.bak and cmdline.bak, respectively. Then remove any special options that might have caused trouble (especially overclocking options). Alternatively, you can restore original copies of these two files, as provided by the standard Raspbian image download.

▒ **Note** Your FAT32 partition (/boot) probably has about 40 MB of free disk space (for a standard Raspbian disk image). Renaming large files, rather than copying them, saves disk space. Consequently, renaming kernel images is preferred over copying. Small files like config.txt or cmdline.txt can be copied as required.

The entire procedure is summarized here:

1. Rename kernel.img to kernel.bak (retain the normal kernel).

2. Rename kernel_emergency.img to kernel.img.

3. Copy config.txt to config.bak.

4. Copy cmdline.txt to cmdline.bak.

5. Edit or restore config.txt and cmdline.txt to original or safe configurations.

Step 5 requires your own judgment. If you have customized hardware, there may be some nonstandard configuration settings that you need to keep (see the previous "Avoid Safe Mode" section). The idea is to simply give your emergency kernel as much chance for success as possible. Disabling all overclocking options is also recommended.

■ **Caution**   After changes, make sure you properly unmount the SD card media (Linux/Mac) or "safely remove USB device" in Windows. Pulling the SD card out before all of the disk data has been written will corrupt your FAT32 partition, adding to your troubles. This may even cause loss of files.

With the kernel exchanged and the configuration restored to safe options, it should now be possible to boot the emergency kernel. Log in and rescue.

To restore your system back to its normal state, you'll need to follow these steps:

1.   Rename kernel.img to kernel_emergency.img (for future rescues).

2.   Rename kernel.bak to kernel.img (reinstate your normal kernel).

3.   Restore/alter your config.txt configuration, if necessary.

4.   Restore/alter your cmdline.txt configuration, if necessary.

At this point, you can reboot with your original kernel and configuration.

CHAPTER 3

Initialization

After the Linux kernel is booted, the first executing userland process ID number (PID) is 1. This process, known as init, is initially responsible for spawning all other required processes required by the system. The init process continues to execute after the system is up, running as a daemon (in the background). It should never be terminated by the user (when attempted on Raspbian Linux, the kill request was ignored).

Run Levels

The init process maintains a concept of a run level for the system. The current run level can be checked at the command line:

```
$ runlevel
N 2
$
```

The N shown here is the previous run level that was in effect. This N means that there was no prior run level. The 2 shown at the right is the current run-level number.

Raspbian Linux supports the run levels shown in Table 3-1. According to the action defined in Raspbian Linux's /etc/inittab file, it changes to run level 2 by default (see the /etc/inittab line with the initdefault action, which is described later). If problems are encountered, such as a corrupted root file system, the run level is taken to *single-user mode* (1). This allows the user at the console to repair the problem and resume the transition to a multiuser run level (normally 2) afterward.

Table 3-1. *Raspbian Run Levels*

Run Level	Meaning	Notes
S or s	Used at initial boot	Reserved
0	Halt	Reserved
1	Single-user mode	Reserved
2	Multiuser mode	Default
3	Multiuser mode	

(*continued*)

Table 3-1. (*continued*)

Run Level	Meaning	Notes
4	Multiuser mode	
5	Multiuser mode	
6	Initiate reboot	Reserved
7	Undocumented	See man 8 init
8	Undocumented	
9	Undocumented	

/etc/inittab

Once the init process has begun and performed its own initialization, it starts reading from configuration file /etc/inittab. This small file has a simple format composed of four fields, separated by colons:

```
id:runlevels:action:process
```

Lines beginning with a # are ignored as comments. Table 3-2 describes the four fields.

Table 3-2. /etc/inittab Fields

Field	Name	Description
1	id	A *unique* 1- to 4-character name for the entry
2	runlevel(s)	Lists the run levels for which the specified action should be performed
3	action	Describes the action required
4	process	Command-line text for the process

inittab Action initdefault

The /etc/inittab file should have one (and only one) entry, with an action named initdefault. This identifies what the initial run level should be after booting. The run level value is taken from the runlevels field of this entry. The Raspbian Linux image uses the following:

```
# The default runlevel .
id:2:initdefault:
```

This specifies that run level 2 is entered after the Linux kernel has booted. The name in the id field is not important here and simply must be unique within the file. The process field is also ignored for this entry. If the /etc/inittab file lacks the initdefault entry, init will ask for a run level from the console.

Field 3 of the inittab line specifies an action. The possible action choices are described in Table 3-3.

Table 3-3. *init Actions*

Action	Description	Notes
respawn	Restart whenever process terminates.	
wait	The process is started once when the run level is entered, and init will wait for its termination.	
once	Process is started when run level is entered.	
boot	Executed during system boot.	Ignores run levels, after sysinit entries
bootwait	Executed during system boot, but waits for the process to complete.	Ignores run levels, after sysinit entries
off	This does nothing (treat as a comment).	
ondemand	Execute upon demand: a, b, or c.	No run-level change
initdefault	Specifies the initial run level to use.	
sysinit	Execute during system boot.	Prior to boot/ bootwait
		Ignores run levels
powerwait	Execute process when power goes down.	Waits for termination
powerfail	Execute process when power goes down.	Does not wait
powerokwait	Execute process when power restored.	
powerfailnow	Execute process when UPS signals near exhaustion of battery.	
ctrlaltdel	Execute process when init sees SIGINT.	SIGINT triggered by Ctrl-Alt-Delete.
kbrequest	Execute process after special key press.	

General Startup Sequence

Ignoring special events like power on demand and keyboard events, the general /etc/inittab processing follows this sequence:

1. /etc/inittab is searched for the initdefault action.

2. The user is prompted at the console for a run level, if none is found in /etc/inittab or the file is missing.

3. The init process sets the run level.

4. The sysinit entries are performed.

5. The boot and bootwait entries are performed.

6. All other entries that include the established run level are performed.

Step 4: sysinit

The standard Raspbian image uses the following for step 4:

```
# Boot-time system configuration/initialization script.
# This is run first except when booting in emergency (-b) mode.
si::sysinit:/etc/init.d/rcS
```

The preceding sysinit entry specifies that script /etc/init.d/rcS is to be run. This is a simple script that redirects the execution to yet another script:

```
#!/bin/sh
#
# rcS
#
# Call all S??* scripts in /etc/rcS.d/ in numerical/alphabetical order
#

exec /etc/init.d/rc S
```

From this we see that execution continues with /etc/init.d/rc with argument 1 set to S. This script is responsible for starting and stopping services on run-level changes. This particular inittab entry is used at initial boot-up and is used to invoke all startup scripts in /etc/rcS.d/S*.

Each of the /etc/rcS.d/S* scripts get invoked with one argument, start. Normally, the script would invoke /etc/rcS.d/K* scripts first (kill scripts that we will discuss later), but upon initial boot, there is no prior run level.

Step 5: boot/bootwait

Under Raspbian Linux, there are no boot or bootwait entries to perform.

Step 6: runlevel

The last step of the initialization involves changing from the non-run-level N to the run level 2, which was declared by the `initdefault` entry. The Raspbian `inittab` declares that the `/etc/init.d/rc` script is run with a run-level argument for each of these run-level changes:

```
l0:0:wait:/etc/init.d/rc 0
l1:1:wait:/etc/init.d/rc 1
l2:2:wait:/etc/init.d/rc 2
l3:3:wait:/etc/init.d/rc 3
l4:4:wait:/etc/init.d/rc 4
l5:5:wait:/etc/init.d/rc 5
l6:6:wait:/etc/init.d/rc 6
```

The first part of starting a new run level is to run the stop (kill) scripts at the *new* run level, provided that there was a previous run level. At boot time, there is no current level (it is N). So at startup, these scripts are ignored.

If, however, the system had been in single-user mode (for example) and the system was changed to run level 2, these kill scripts would be invoked:

```
$ ls -lL /etc/rc2.d/K*
-rwxr-xr-x 1 root root 2610 Jul  25 2011 /etc/rc2.d/K01lightdm
-rwxr-xr-x 1 root root 6491 Jul  21 2012 /etc/rc2.d/K05nfs-common
-rwxr-xr-x 1 root root 2344 Jun  15 2012 /elc/rc2.d/K05rpcbind
```

The script `/etc/init.d/rc` first iterates through these kill scripts (in sort order). When the current level has a stop (kill) script, the following logic applies:

1. If the previous run level *did* have a matching stop (kill) script, and

2. If the previous level *didn't* have a start script,

3. *Then there is no need to execute the stop (kill) script.*

Otherwise, the corresponding kill script is necessary and is performed.

At startup, or after a run-level change, the startup scripts for the new run level (2 in this example) are performed. When the current level has a start script, then the following logic applies:

1. If the previous run level *also* has a matching start script, and

2. The current level *doesn't* have a stop (kill) script,

3. *Then there is no need to stop and restart the script.*

Otherwise, the start script is invoked.

For all run levels except 0 and 6, the action being performed by the /etc/init.d/rc
script is to *start* services (except where kill scripts apply). Entering run level 0 (halt) or 6
(reboot) is a bit different, since the script must be *stopping* services.

The following is an example list of startup scripts used by the Raspberry Pi when
entering run level 2 after booting:

```
$ ls -lL /etc/rc2.d/S*
-rwxr-xr-x 1 root root 1276 Aug 31 2012   /etc/rc2.d/S01bootlogs
-rwxr-xr-x 1 root root 4698 May  1 2012   /etc/rc2.d/S01ifplugd
-rwxr-xr-x 1 root root  995 Aug 31 2012   /etc/rc2.d/S01motd
-rwxr-xr-x 1 root root 3054 Sep 26 2012   /etc/rc2.d/S01rsyslog
-rwxr-xr-x 1 root root  714 Jun 28 2012   /etc/rc2.d/S01sudo
-rwxr-xr-x 1 root root 3169 May 10 2011   /etc/rc2.d/S01triggerhappy
-rwxr-xr-x 1 root root 3033 Jul  9 2012   /etc/rc2.d/S02cron
-rwxr-xr-x 1 root root 2832 Sep 29 2012   /etc/rc2.d/S02dbus
-rwxr-xr-x 1 root root 2148 Jun  9 2012   /etc/rc2.d/S02dphys-swapfile
-rwxr-xr-x 1 root root 1814 Dec 26 2009   /etc/rc2.d/S02ntp
-rwxr-xr-x 1 root root 4395 Dec 13 06:43 /etc/rc2.d/S02rsync
-rwxr-xr-x 1 root root 3881 Feb 24 2012   /etc/rc2.d/S02ssh
-rwxr-xr-x 1 root root 1313 Jun 30 2012   /etc/rc2.d/S04plymouth
-rwxr-xr-x 1 root root  782 Mar 16 2012   /etc/rc2.d/S04rc.local
-rwxr-xr-x 1 root root 1074 Mar 16 2012   /etc/rc2.d/S04rmnologin
```

Like many Linux distributions, Raspbian Linux places the actual script files in the
directory /etc/init.d. The names found in /etc/rc2.d, for example, are symlinks to the
actual files.

It should also be noted that these scripts are run in the order determined by the pair
of digits following the S or K prefix. This is a natural consequence of the way the shell sorts
file names when listing files.

inittab Action wait

The wait init action is useful for entries that you want to run individually when the new
run level is first entered. The init process will not resume with further entries until the
launched process has terminated (whether launched successfully or not). Presumably,
there is an implied order based on line sequence found in the file. An important attribute
of this type of entry is that it is performed only *once* upon starting the run level.

inittab Action once

The once action is very similar to the wait action, except that the init process will *not*
wait for the started process to terminate (perhaps it doesn't). Entries marked once are
started only once per entry of a given run level, but init then proceeds with immediately
processing other entries.

inittab Action respawn

The respawn option is often used for processes that manage terminal lines (gettys). The following example is taken from the standard Raspbian /etc/inittab:

```
# Spawn a getty on Raspberry Pi serial line
T0:23:respawn:/sbin/getty -L ttyAMA0 115200 vt100
```

This entry is used whenever init enters run levels 2 or 3. It launches program /sbin/getty to prompt the user for login on the serial console device (/dev/ttyAMA0 in this example). Other command-line parameters help the getty program to configure the terminal and login environment. When the user logs out of his session, the getty process terminates. When init notices that the process has terminated, it starts /sbin/getty again because of the respawn action. In this way, the terminal line is readied for the next user login.

▓ **Caution** When using the respawn action for your own application, be careful that it doesn't fail frequently. Otherwise, init will churn by repeatedly restarting your process after it fails. You may eventually get a message on the console with init temporarily suspending the entry. This reduces the hogging of system resources from frequent respawning. But this suspension is temporary.

Changing Run Levels

The preceding sections outlined the startup procedure. Let's now examine what happens when you change run levels.

telinit

The /sbin/telinit executable is linked to the init program file /sbin/init. This form of the command is used to inform the executing init process to request a change of run levels:

```
# telinit x
```

where x is the new run level to enter. The run level may be specified only as one of the choices described in Table 3-4.

Table 3-4. *telinit Run Levels*

Level	Description
0-6	Run level 0, 1, 2, 3, 4, 5, or 6
a, b, c	Invoke inittab entries with a, b, or c
Q or q	Tell init to reexamine /etc/inittab
S or s	Change to single-user mode
U or u	Tell init to reexecute itself

Any unrecognized level is silently ignored.

Change of Run Level

Let's use an example to keep the references concrete. If you were in run level 1 and directed the system to change to run level 2 with

```
# telinit  2
```

the following happens:

1. /etc/init.d/rc executes all K* (kill) scripts for run level 2 (the level you are changing to), with an argument of stop.

2. /etc/init.d/rc executes all S* (start) scripts for run level 2, with the argument start.

3. Except where previously noted (redundant stop and start script executions are omitted)

Another way to think about this is that all K* symlinks at a particular run level identify services that *should not be running* at that level. Similarly, the S* symlinks identify services that *should be running* at that level.

Single-User Mode

Changing to single-user mode works the same as for any other level, except that most of the scripts are designed to be kill scripts to stop services (/etc/rc1.d/K*), rather than to start them.

The concept of single-user mode is that only one user will be using the system, without unnecessary services running in the background. This run level is normally used to repair the file systems or to reconfigure the system.

Halt and Reboot

Changing to level 0 (halt) or 6 (reboot) requires stopping all services. As a result, in this case only the kill scripts are performed with the argument stop. In the file

```
/usr/share/doc/sysv-rc/README.runlevels
```

you will find this remark:

In the future, the /etc/rc6.d/SXXxxxx scripts MIGHT be moved to /etc/rc6.d/ K1XXxxxx for clarity."

Creating a New Service

If you had a dedicated application for your Raspberry Pi, you might want to assign it to a dedicated run level, perhaps 4. In this manner, you could still perform maintenance and perhaps even development in run level 2. When it was time to start the dedicated application, you'd use telinit to change to run level 4. You could even have /etc/inittab cause a reboot directly into level 4, by the following entry:

```
id:4:initdefault:
```

Rebooting directly to your custom run level 4 would be useful for solar applications to handle restarts due to power fluctuations.

To arrange the startup/kill scripts, you would need the following:

1. Kill scripts at the following locations (symlinks to /etc/init.d/service). These apply when you change from level 4 to one of the other levels, where you don't want the service running.

    a. /etc/rc2.d/KXXservice

    b. /etc/rc3.d/KXXservice

    c. /etc/rc5.d/KXXservice

    d. Note that single-user mode by default will not have other services left running.

2. You will need a startup script for run level 4:

    a. /etc/rc4.d/SXXservice

In the preceding script, XX is a sequence number (00 to 99) that positions where in the list of scripts it gets executed.

Also note that the symlinks

- /etc/rc2.d/KXXservice

- /etc/rc2.d/SXXservice

point to the same file in /etc/init.d/service. The K* symlinks are invoked with the argument stop, while the S* symlinks are invoked with start. This means that your single /etc/init.d/service script file should stop or start based on this command-line argument.

The advantage of running your dedicated application from its own run level includes the following:

- Less competition for CPU resources from unused daemons

- Increased security by not running services that permit external login attempts

- Restricted physical access—login only via the serial port console (when configured)

- Automatic restart of your application after a power failure

With run levels 3, 4, and 5 to work with, you can configure a mix of different dedicated application profiles.

CHAPTER 4

vcgencmd

Apart from the usual Linux commands that display status, the Raspberry Pi includes a custom command named vcgencmd, which can report voltages and temperatures. This chapter documents the known features of the command.

The executable file behind the command is /usr/bin/vcgencmd.

vcgencmd Commands

There is no man page for this command, but the list of all supported options can be displayed with the commands option. The command output has been broken over several lines for readability:

```
$ vcgencmd commands
commands="vcos, ap_output_control, ap_output_post_processing, \
pm_set_policy, pm_get_status, pm_show_stats, pm_start_logging, \
pm_stop_logging, version, commands, set_vll_dir, \
led_control, set_backlight, set_logging, get_lcd_info, \
set_bus_arbiter_mode, cache_flush, otp_dump, codec_enabled, \
measure_clock, measure_volts, measure_temp, get_config, \
hdmi_ntsc_freqs, render_bar, disk_notify, inuse_notify, \
sus_suspend, sus_status, sus_is_enabled, \
sus_stop_test_thread, egl_platform_switch, mem_validate, \
mem_oom, mem_reloc_stats, file, vctest_memmap, vctest_start, \
vctest_stop, vctest_set, vctest_get"
```

At the time of this writing, some of these options remained undocumented. A summary list of options is itemized in Table 4-1.

Table 4-1. *Summary of vcgencmd Command-Line Options*

Option Name	Argument(s)	Description
ap_output_control		
ap_output_post_processing		
cache_flush		Flushes GPU's L1 cache
codec_enabled	codec	Reports status of codec
commands		Lists options
disk_notify		
egl_platform_switch		
file		
get_config		
get_lcd_info		Returns height, width, and depth of the display frame buffer
hdmi_ntsc_freqs		
inuse_notify		
led_control		
measure_clock	clock	Reports frequency
measure_temp		Reports SoC temperature
measure_volts	device	Reports voltage
mem_oom		Reports Out of Memory events
mem_reloc_stats		Reports relocatable memory stats
mem_validate		
otp_dump		
pm_get_status		
pm_set_policy		
pm_show_stats		
pm_start_logging		
pm_stop_logging		
render_bar		
set_backlight		
set_bus_arbiter_mode		
set_logging		

Option measure_clock

This firmware access option provides the user with clock rate information, according to the argument appearing after measure_clock. Valid values for *<clock>* are listed in Table 4-2.

```
vcgencmd  measure_clock  <clock>
```

Table 4-2. *Valid Arguments for the measure_clock Option*

Clock	Description
arm	ARM CPU
core	Core
dpi	Display Pixel Interface
emmc	External MMC device
h264	h.264 encoder
hdmi	HDMI clock
isp	Image Sensor Pipeline
pixel	Pixel clock
pwm	Pulse Width Modulation
uart	UART clock
v3d	Video 3D
vec	

The following shell script is often used to list all available clocks:

```
$ for src in arm core h264 isp v3d uart pwm emmc pixel vec hdmi dpi ; do
  echo -e "$src : $(vcgencmd measure_clock $src)" ;
done
```

Here is the example output:

```
arm   :    frequency (45)=700074000
core  :    frequency (1)=250000000
h264  :    frequency (28)=250000000
isp   :    frequency (42)=250000000
v3d   :    frequency (43)=250000000
uart  :    frequency (22)=3000000
pwm   :    frequency (25)=0
emmc  :    frequency (47)=100000000
```

```
pixel :   frequency (29)=108000000
vec   :   frequency (10)=0
hdmi  :   frequency (9)=163683000
dpi   :   frequency (4)=0
```

Option measure_volts

The measure_volts option allows the various subsystem voltages to be reported:

```
$ for id in core sdram_c sdram_i sdram_p ; do
  echo -e "$id: $(vcgencmd measure_volts $id)" ;
done
core    :   volt=1.20V
sdram_c:   volt=1.20V
sdram_i:   volt=1.20V
sdram_p:   volt=1.23V
```

Table 4-3 provides a legend for the output report lines.

Table 4-3. *Valid Device Names for measure_volts*

Device	Description
core	Core
sdram_c	SDRAM controller
sdram_i	SDRAM I/O
sdram_p	SDRAM physical

Option measure_temp

The measure_temp option allows the user to retrieve the SoC temperature, in degrees Celsius.

```
$ vcgencmd measure_temp
temp=36.3 °C
```

In this example, the relatively idle core was reported to be 36.3°C.

Option codec_enabled

The codec_enabled option reports the operational status of the codecs supported by the Raspberry Pi. Valid codec names are listed in Table 4-4. The codec support can be summarized with the following command:

```
$ for id in H264 MPG2WCV1 ; do
  echo -e "$id: $(vcgencmd codec_enabled $id)";
done
H264:    H264=enabled
MPG2:    MPG2=disabled
WCV1:    WCV1=disabled
```

Table 4-4. *vcgencmd CODEC Names*

Name	Description
H264	h.264 CODEC
MPG2	MPEG-2 CODEC
WVC1	VC1 CODEC

Option version

The version option reports the GPU firmware version:

```
$ vcgencmd version
Oct 25 2012 16:37:21
Copyright (c) 2012 Broadcom
version 346337 (release)
```

Option get_lcd_info

While get_lcd_info was undocumented at the time of this writing, it appears to provide LCD/monitor width and height, and pixel depth:

```
$ vcgencmd get_lcd_info
720 480 24
```

Option get_config

The get_config option is useful in scripts that need to query your Raspberry Pi's configuration, as defined in /boot/config.txt. See Chapter 2 for the options that can be queried. For example, a script can query whether avoid_safe_mode is in effect:

```
$ vcgencmd get_config avoid_safe_mode
avoid_safe_mode=0
```

CHAPTER 5

Linux Console

The Raspbian Linux console is configured (or assumed) by the kernel command line. See the console option described in Chapter 2.

Available Consoles

The list of consoles is available through the /proc/consoles pseudo file:

```
$ cat /proc/consoles
tty1                      -WU (EC p )     4:1
ttyAMA0                   -W- (E  p )   204:64
```

The organization and flags displayed are described in Tables 5-1 and 5-2. The major and minor numbers are confirmed in the following example session output:

```
$ ls -l /dev/tty1 /dev/ttyAMA0
crw-rw---- 1 root tty   4,   1 Jan 21 00:06 /dev/tty1
crw-rw---- 1 root tty 204,  64 Jan 21 00:06 /dev/ttyAMA0
```

Table 5-1. /proc/consoles Fields

Field	Parameter	Example	Description
1	device	tty1	/dev/tty1
2	operations	-WU-	R = read
			W = write
			U = unblank
3	flags	(EC p)	See flags in Table 5-2
4	major:minor	4:1	Device major/minor

Table 5-2. *The Meaning of Flags Displayed in Parentheses*

Flag	Meaning
E	The console is enabled.
C	Is the preferred console.
B	Primary boot console.
p	Used for printk buffer.
b	Not a TTY, but is a Braille device.
a	Safe to use when CPU is offline.

Serial Console

If you wired up a serial console to your Raspberry Pi, you can use a utility such as PuTTY (http://www.chiark.greenend.org.uk/~sgtatham/putty/download.html) on your laptop or desktop computer to connect to it. The serial console sees the following first few lines at boot (long lines are edited):

```
Uncompressing Linux… done, booting the kernel.
[ 0.000000] Initializing cgroup subsys cpu
[ 0.000000] Linux version 3.2.27+  (dc4@dc4-arm-01) \
  (gcc version 4.7.2 20120731 (prerelease) \
  (crosstool -NG linaro -1.13.1+bzr2458 - Linaro GCC 2012.08 )) \
  #250 PREEMPT Thu Oct 18 19:03:02 BST 2012
[ 0.000000] CPU: ARMv6-compatible processor [410fb767] \
  revision 7 (ARMv7), cr=00c5387d
[ 0.000000]  CPU : PIPT /VIPT nonaliasing data cache, \
  VIPT nonaliasing instruction cache
[ 0.000000]  Machine:  BCM2708
```

Using the dmesg command, you can see almost the same thing:

```
$ dmesg | head -5
[ 0.000000] Initializing cgroup subsys cpu
[ 0.000000] Linux version 3.2.27+ (dc4@dc4-arm-01) \
  (gcc version 4.7.2 20120731 (prerelease) \
  (crosstool -NG linaro -1.13.1+bzr2458 - Linaro GCC 2012.08)) \
  #250 PREEMPT Thu Oct 18 19:03:02 BST 2012
[ 0.000000] CPU: ARMv6-compatible processor [410fb767] \
  revision 7 (ARMv7), cr=00c5387d
[ 0.000000] CPU:PIPT/VIPT nonaliasing data cache, \
  VIPT nonaliasing instruction cache
[ 0.000000] Machine:BCM2708
```

The difference is that the initial Uncompressing Linux console output is missing. Additionally, any debug messages that a new kernel might display can be capturable on a serial console.

CHAPTER 6

Cross-Compiling

Embedded computers often lack the necessary resources for developing and compiling software. The Raspberry Pi is rather special in this regard since it already includes the gcc compiler and the needed linking tools (under Raspbian Linux). But while the code can be developed and built on the Raspberry Pi, it may not always be the most suitable place for software development. One reason is the lower performance of the SD card.

To compile *native* code for the Raspberry Pi, you need a compiler and linker that knows how to generate ARM binary executables. Yet it must run on a host with a different architecture (for example, Mac OS X). Hence the reason it is called a *cross*-compiler. The cross-compiler will take your source code on the local (build) platform and generate ARM binary executables, to be installed on your target Pi.

There are prebuilt cross-compile tools available, including the Raspberry Pi Foundation's own tools (git://github.com/raspberrypi/tools.git), but these can be problematic for some versions of Linux. Running the cross-compiler on a different Linux release than it was built for may cause the software to complain about missing or incompatible shared libraries. But if you find that you can use a prebuilt release, it will save considerable time.

In this chapter, you'll walk through how to build your own cross-compiler. This may permit you to get the job done using your existing Linux release.

Terminology

Let's first cover some terminology used in this chapter:

> *build*: Also called the *local* platform, this is the platform that you perform the compiling on (for example, Mac OS X).

> *target*: The destination platform, which is the Raspberry Pi (ARM) in this chapter.

Let's now consider some of the cross-compiling issues before you take the plunge. There are two main problem areas in cross-compiling:

- All C/C++ include files and libraries for the Raspberry Pi (ARM) must be available on your build platform.

- The cross-compiler and related tools must generate code suitable for the target platform

So before you decide that you want to build a cross-compiler environment, are you prepared to

- Provide all matching C/C++ header files from the ARM platform?

- Provide all ARM libraries needed, including libraries for third-party products like sqlite3 that you intend to link with?

- Provide sufficient disk space for the cross-compiler and tools?

The crosstool-NG software will mitigate some of these issues. For example, the correct Linux headers are chosen by the configuration step shown later in this chapter.

Disk space solves many issues by holding a copy of your Raspberry Pi's root file system on your build platform. Simple programs won't require this (for example, a Hello World). But software linking to libraries may require this. Even if you're strapped for disk space, you may be able to mount the Raspbian SD card on the build platform, thus gaining access to the Raspberry Pi's root file system.

Operating System

The procedure used for building a cross-compiler environment is somewhat complex and fragile. Using the crosstool-NG software simplifies things considerably. Despite this advantage, it is best to stick with proven cross-compiler platforms and configurations.

You might be tempted to say, "The source code is open, and so it should work on just about any operating system." (You might even say, "I'll fix the problems myself.") The reality is not quite so simple. I use the Mac Ports collection (`www.macports.org`) for a number of things and quickly discovered the limitations of building a crosstool-NG on Mac OS X. For example, I found that objcopy was not supported when `./configure` was run for the cross-compiler. Unless you are willing to spend time on Internet forums and wait for answers, I suggest you take a more pragmatic approach—build your cross-compiling environment on a recent and stable Ubuntu or Debian environment.

This chapter uses Ubuntu 14.04 LTS hosted in VirtualBox 4.3.12 (`www.virtualbox.org`) on a Mac OS X Mavericks MacBook Pro, running an Intel i7 processor. Current versions of Ubuntu are recommended. Ubuntu 12.10 was the version tested and used by the process documented at this link:

`www.kitware.com/blog/home/post/426`

Host, Guest, Build, and Target

At this point, a short note is in order because these terms can get confusing, especially for those performing this for the first time. Let's list the environment terms, which will be referred to throughout the remainder of this chapter:

- *Host* environment

- *Guest* environment

- *Build/local* environment

- *Target* environment

So many environments! The terms *host* and *guest* environments enter the picture when you are using a virtual machine like VirtualBox. VirtualBox is used to *host*" another operating system on top of the one you are using. For example, you might be running Mac OS X on your laptop. In this example, the OS X environment *hosts* Ubuntu Linux within VirtualBox. The Ubuntu Linux operating system is thus referred to as the *guest* operating system.

The term *build* (or *local*) environment refers to the Linux environment that is executing the cross-compiler and tools. These Linux tools produce or manipulate code for the *target* environment (your Raspberry Pi's ARM CPU).

Platform Limitations

Many people today are using 64-bit platforms similar to my own MacBook Pro, with an Intel i7 processor. This may present a problem if you want to build a cross-compiler for the Raspberry Pi, which is a 32-bit platform. Many people building a cross-compiler on a 64-bit platform have encountered software problems building for a 32-bit platform.

For this reason, if you are using a 64-bit platform, you'll probably want to choose a VirtualBox solution. This will allow you to run a 32-bit operating system to host the cross-compiler. On the other hand, if you are already running a 32-bit operating system, creating a native cross-compiler for the Pi is a real possibility.

Without VirtualBox (Native)

If you are already using a Linux development environment like Debian or Ubuntu, the term *host* is equivalent to the build (or local) environment. The host and guest environments are likewise equivalent, though it is probably more correct to say there is no guest operating system in this scenario. This simpler scenario leaves us with just two environments:

> *Host/guest/build*: Native environment running the cross-compiler tools

> *Target*: The destination execution environment (Raspberry Pi)

Using VirtualBox (Ubuntu/Linux)

If you do not have a suitable Linux environment, one can be hosted on the platform you have. You can host Linux from Windows, Mac OS X, Solaris, or another distribution of Linux. VirtualBox can be downloaded from the following:

www.virtualbox.org

When VirtualBox is used, the *host* environment is the environment that is running VirtualBox (for example, Mac OS X). The *guest* operating system will be Ubuntu (recommended) or Debian. This leaves us with three environments in total:

Host: Or native, running VirtualBox (for example, Windows)

Guest/build: Ubuntu/Debian development environment within VirtualBox

Target: The destination execution environment (your Raspberry Pi)

Planning Your Cross-Development Environment

The main consideration at this point is normally disk space. If you are using VirtualBox, limited memory can be another factor. If you are using Linux or Mac OS X, check your mounted disks for available space (or Windows tools as appropriate):

```
$ df -k
Filesystem      1024-blocks   Used        Available  Capacity  Mounted on
/dev/disk0s2    731734976     154168416   577310560  22%       /
devfs           186           186         0          100%      /dev
map -hosts      0             0           0          100%      /net
map auto_home   0             0           0          100%      /home
map -static     0             0           0          100%      /Volumes/oth
$
```

In the preceding example output, we see that the root file system has plenty of space. But your file system may be laid out differently. Symlinks can be used when necessary to graft a larger disk area onto your home directory.

If you're using VirtualBox, create virtual disks with enough space for the Linux operating system and your cross-compiler environment. You may want to put your Linux software on one virtual disk with a minimum size of about 8–10 GB (allow it to grow larger).

Allow a minimum of 10 GB for your cross-compiler environment (and allow it to grow). 9 GB is just barely large enough to host the cross-compiler tools and allow you to compile a Hello World type of program. But you must also factor in additional space for the Raspberry Linux kernel, its include files, and all other third-party libraries that you might need to build with (better still, a copy of the Raspberry Pi's root file system).

Within your development Ubuntu/Debian build environment, make sure your cross-compiler and build area are using the disk area that has available space. It is easy to glibly create a directory someplace convenient and find out later that the space that you thought you were going to use wasn't available.

Building the Cross-Compiler

At this point, I'll assume that you've set up and installed Ubuntu in VirtualBox, if necessary. Otherwise, you are building your cross-compiler tools on an existing Ubuntu/Debian system, with disk space sufficient for the job.

We will be using the basic recipe outlined from this web resource:

"Cross-Compiling for Raspberry Pi," www.kitware.com/blog/home/post/426

Download crosstool-NG

The released crosstool-NG downloads are found at this site:

```
http://crosstool-ng.org/download/crosstool-ng/
    current release: crosstool-ng-1.19.0.tar.bz2
```

It is normal practice to download the newest stable version of software. I am using 1.19.0 in this text because it was current at the time of writing.

Staging Directory

I'll assume that you've symlinked to your disk area with sufficient available disk space. In other words, the symlink named ~/devel points to the development area to be used. This can be just a subdirectory if you have sufficient disk space there.

In directory ~/devel, create a subdirectory named staging (~/devel/staging) and change it to the following:

```
$ cd ~/devel      # Dir is ~/devel
$ mkdir staging
$ cd ./staging    # Dir is ~/devel/staging
$ pwd
/home/myuserid/devel/staging
$
```

Unpack the Tarball

Assuming the tarball crosstool-ng-1.19.0.tar.bz2 was downloaded to your home directory, you would perform the following (change the option j if the suffix is not .bz2):

```
$ tar xjvf ~/crosstool-ng-1.19.0.tar.bz2
. . .
$
```

After the unpacking completes, you should have a subdirectory named crosstoolng-1.19.0 in your staging directory.

Create /opt/x-tools

You can choose a different location if you like, but I'm going to assume that the crosstool-NG software is going to install into /opt/x-tools. We'll also assume your user ID is fred (substitute your own).

```
$ sudo mkdir -p /opt/x-tools
$ sudo chown fred /opt/x-tools
```

Once your installation is complete later, you can change the ownership back to root for protection.

Install Package Dependencies

The crosstool-NG build depends on several packages provided by Ubuntu/Debian as optionally installed software:

> bison: GNU yacc
>
> flex: GNU lex
>
> subversion: Subversion source control package
>
> libtool: Library tool
>
> texinfo: Install the texinfo package
>
> gawk: GNU awk (gawk)
>
> gperf: Perfect hash function generator
>
> automake: Tool for generating GNU standards-compliant Makefiles

Save time by making sure these packages are installed before proceeding to the next step. Package dependencies often change over time. Depending on your host system, you may find that additional packages (such as libncurses5-dev, for example) are also needed. If more packages are needed, the configure step usually identifies them.

Configure crosstools-NG

With the package dependencies installed, you are now in a position to make the crosstool-NG software:

```
$ cd ~/devel/staging/crosstool-ng-1.19.0
$ ./configure --prefix=/opt/x-tools
```

If this completes without errors, you are ready to build and install the crosstool-NG software. If it reports that you are missing package dependencies, install them now and repeat.

make crosstool-ng

At this point, you should have no trouble building crosstool-NG. Perform the following make command:

```
$ cd ~/devel/staging/crosstool-ng-1.19.0
$ make
```

This takes very little time and seems trouble free.

make install

Once the crosstool-NG package has been compiled, it is ready to be installed into /opt/x-tools. From the same directory:

```
$ sudo make install
```

If you still own the directory /opt/x-tools from earlier (recall sudo chown fred /opt/x-tools), you won't need to use sudo in the preceding step. After make install is performed, you will have the crosstool-NG command ct-ng installed in the directory /opt/x-tools/bin.

PATH

To use the newly installed ct-ng command, you will need to adjust your PATH environment variable:

```
$ PATH="/opt/x-tools/bin:$PATH"
```

The website also indicates that you might have to unset environment variable LD_LIBRARY_PATH, if your platform has it defined. If so, then unset it as follows:

```
$ unset LD_LIBRARY_PATH
```

Now you should be able to run ct-ng to get version info (note that there are no hyphens in front of version in the following command). Seeing the version output confirms that your ct-ng command has been installed and is functional:

```
$ ct-ng version
```

This is crosstool-NG version 1.19.0

```
Copyright (C) 2008  Yann E. MORIN <yann.morin.1998@free.fr>
This is free software; see the source for copying conditions.
There is NO warranty; not even for MERCHANTABILITY or FITNESS FOR A
PARTICULAR PURPOSE.
```

Cross-Compiler Configuration

The command ct-ng simplifies the work necessary to configure and build the cross-compiler tool chain. From here, we are concerned with building the cross-compiler tools themselves. When that process is completed, you will have populated the cross-compiler tools into the directory /opt/x-tools/arm-unknown-linux-gnueabi.

Before ct-ng can build your cross-compiler, it must first be configured:

```
$ cd ~/devel/staging
$ ct-ng menuconfig
```

If you get a "command not found" error message, check that the PATH variable is set properly.

Paths and Misc Options

When the command starts up, the menu configuration screen is presented.

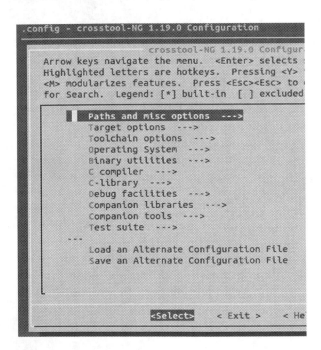

Press Enter, to open the Paths and Misc Options submenu.

Once in the Paths and Misc Options menu, as shown next, use the cursor key to move down to Try Features Marked as Experimental. Once that line is highlighted, press the spacebar to put an asterisk inside the square brackets, to select the option (pressing space again toggles the setting).

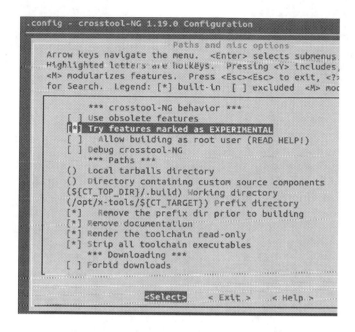

After doing that, while in the same menu, move the cursor down to the middle entry labelled Prefix Directory and press Enter to select it.

For the procedure used in this book, modify the path to the following:

/opt/x-tools/${CT_TARGET}

as illustrated here:

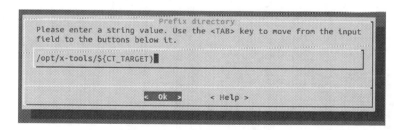

Once the pathname is established, press Enter on the OK button shown. This returns you to the Paths and Misc Options menu.

Then select the Exit button shown at the bottom, and press Enter again.

Target Options

From the main menu, select Target Options with the cursor and press Enter to open that menu. Then choose Target Architecture and press Enter. In that menu, choose Arm and use the Select button at the bottom. This returns you to the Target Options menu.

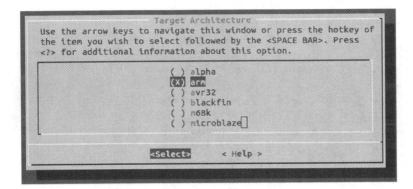

While in the Target Options menu (shown next), verify the Endianness setting by reviewing the status in brackets. It should read Little Endian. If not, enter that menu and change it to *Little endian*. Below the Endianness menu item is the Bitness option. It should already indicate 32-bit. If not, select it and change the setting to 32-bit.

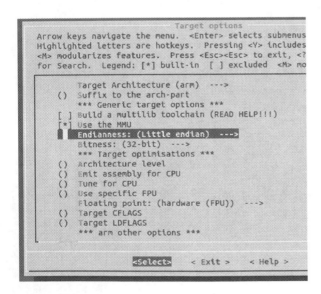

Finally, exit this submenu with the Exit button.

Operating System

At the main menu again, choose Operating System and then choose Linux Kernel Version.

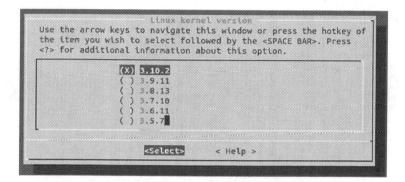

It is best to choose the release that most closely matches the kernel that you are using (perhaps, for example, 3.10.2). Once you have chosen, exit back to the main menu.

Binary Utilities

At the main menu, open the Binary Utilities menu. Cursor down to Binutils Version and open that submenu:

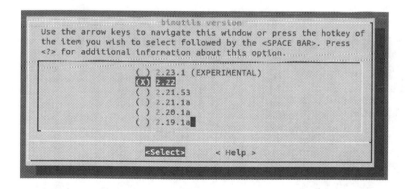

In this menu, you are presented various versions of binutils that can be used. Choose the most current stable (nonexperimental) version. Version 2.22 was chosen here. Select the version and exit back to the main menu.

C Compiler

At the main menu, open the C Compiler submenu. Here it is recommended that you enable the Show Linaro Versions option.

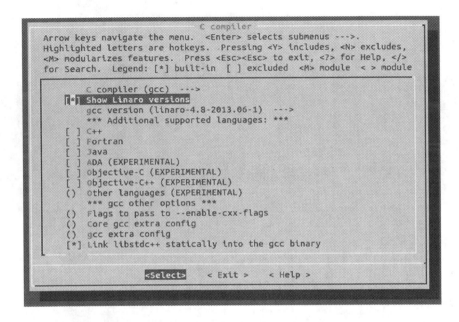

Once that is enabled, you can select the submenu Gcc Version:

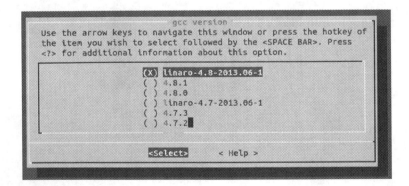

The preceding figure shows linaro-4.8.2013.06-1 being chosen (which I had good results with). Newer versions are always becoming available. Choose the compiler and then choose the Select button at the bottom.

Then choose Exit once again to return to the main menu.

Save Configuration

Unless you have a reason to change anything else, exit the menu again to cause the Save prompt to appear:

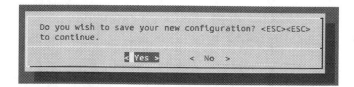

Upon selecting Yes, the command exits with the following session output showing in the terminal window:

```
$ ct-ng menuconfig
  IN    config.gen/arch.in
  IN    config.gen/kernel.in
  IN    config.gen/cc.in
  IN    config.gen/libc.in
  IN    config/config.in
#
# configuration saved
#
```

At this point, it is worth mentioning that you may want to save your configuration somewhere outside the current directory. The configuration is saved in a file named .config and can be copied elsewhere. The following is a suggestion:

```
$ cp .config ~/ct-ng.config.bak
```

Saving the file outside the current directory will prevent accidental loss if ct-ng distclean is invoked.

Build Cross-Compiler

Check the ownership of /opt/x-tools. If you don't own this directory, change the ownership now:

```
$ sudo chown -R fred /opt/x-tools
```

This will save you from having to execute the build process with root privileges. Now at long last, you can initiate the building of the cross-compiler:

```
$ cd ~/devel/staging
$ ct-ng build
```

Allow a good block of time for this job. This is not something that can be pushed through in a hurry. Ideally, you can just leave the command to run and check for successful completion in an hour or so. However, it is not uncommon for different software problems to arise at this stage. I once spent an entire Saturday troubleshooting this step. If you do encounter problems, read the next section for some troubleshooting tips.

If all goes well, ct-ng compiles and installs tools into /opt/x-tools without any further interaction. In the following session, Retrieving needed toolchain components is rather brief, because this was a session rerun with the components cached somewhere. Your download times will be longer when doing this for the first time.

```
[INFO]    Performing some trivial sanity checks
[INFO]    Build started 20140103.102402
[INFO]    Building environment variables
[INFO]    =============================================================
[INFO]    Retrieving needed toolchain components' tarballs
[INFO]    Retrieving needed toolchain components' tarballs: done in 0.13s (at 00:04)
[INFO]    =============================================================
[INFO]    Extracting and patching toolchain components
[INFO]    Extracting and patching toolchain components: done in 3.96s (at 00:08)
[INFO]    =============================================================
[INFO]    Installing GMP for host
[INFO]    Installing GMP for host: done in 37.57s (at 00:46)
[INFO]    =============================================================
[INFO]    Installing MPFR for host
[INFO]    Installing MPFR for host: done in 18.16s (at 01:04)
[INFO]    =============================================================
[INFO]    Installing PPL for host
[INFO]    Installing PPL for host: done in 268.27s (at 05:32)
[INFO]    =============================================================
[INFO]    Installing CLooG/PPL for host
[INFO]    Installing CLooG/PPL for host: done in 6.45s (at 05:39)
[INFO]    =============================================================
[INFO]    Installing MPC for host
[INFO]    Installing MPC for host: done in 7.97s (at 05:47)
[INFO]    =============================================================
[INFO]    Installing binutils for host
[INFO]    Installing binutils for host: done in 53.52s (at 06:40)
[INFO]    =============================================================
[INFO]    Installing pass -1 core C compiler
[INFO]    Installing pass -1 core C compiler: done in 222.36s (at 10:23)
[INFO]    =============================================================
[INFO]    Installing kernel headers
[INFO]    Installing kernel headers: done in 4.54s (at 10:27)
[INFO]    =============================================================
```

```
[INFO]    Installing C library headers & start files
[INFO]    Installing C library headers & start files: done in 31.26s (at 10:58)
[INFO]    ==============================================================
[INFO]    Installing pass -2 core C compiler
[INFO]    Installing pass -2 core C compiler: done in 512.54s (at 19:31)
[INFO]    ==============================================================
[INFO]    Installing C library
[INFO]    Installing C library: done in 805.58s (at 32:57)
[INFO]    ==============================================================
[INFO]    Installing final compiler
[INFO]    Installing final compiler: done in 484.58s (at 41:01)
[INFO]    ==============================================================
[INFO]    Cleaning -up the toolchain's directory
[INFO]    Stripping all toolchain executables
[INFO]    Cleaning -up the toolchain's directory: done in 3.86s (at 41:05)
[INFO]    Build completed at 20130103.110507
[INFO]    (elapsed: 41:04.93)
[INFO]    Finishing installation (may take a few seconds )...
[41:05]   /
```

The overall time for my build was 41 minutes (reported to be 83 minutes on a Windows 8 Intel i5 using VirtualBox). My build was performed in VirtualBox running on Mac OS X Mavericks, using the Intel i7 processor (2.8 GHz). On the same Mac, I found that the times approximately doubled when the VirtualBox disk images were located on a USB 2.0 disk drive. From these figures, you can estimate your build time.

Troubleshooting

The session output that you get from this build process is very terse. As such, you don't always get a clear idea of what the real failure was. For this reason, you'll often need to check the build.log file:

```
$ less build.log
```

Using less, you can navigate to the end of the build.log file by typing a capital G.
One failure that frequently occurs in the beginning is a *failed download*. While the build process does retry downloads and tries different download methods, it can still fail. All that you need to do is to start the build again. It will download only the remaining files needed. Sometimes it will succeed on the second or third retry attempt.

Sometimes a component will fail in its *configuration phase*. Check the build.log file first to determine precisely which component is involved. Next you will want to examine the config.log file for that particular component. For example, let's say the isl component failed. Dive down into the .build subdirectory until you find its config.log file:

```
$ cd .build/arm-unknown-linux-gnueabi/build/build-isl-host-i686-build_pc-
linux-gnu
$ less config.log
```

Navigate to the end of config.log and work backward a few pages. Eventually, you will see text describing the command that was tried and the error message produced. In one instance, I was able to determine that the custom compiler option that I added (-fpermissive) was causing the failure. The solution then was to remove that option and try again.

Some errors will occur only with certain version choices. At one time, I was receiving errors related to PPL and needed a patch to correct it. Google is your friend (the following patch is an example):

```
http://patchwork.ozlabs.org/patch/330733/
```

I found that saving that patch to a file and applying it to the sources corrected the issue. Later, when I decided to start over with a different choice of compiler, this patch became unnecessary (the software was downloaded fresh again).

In getting through these issues, you can simply make corrections and then rerun the ct-ng build command. It is recommended that you plan for a later rebuild of everything again (after a clean), once the problems are solved. This will ensure that you have a good build without dependency issues.

If, after a correction, you run into the same problem, you may need to do a clean step first and start over. Depending on how deep you think the problem may be, choose one of the following:

- ct-ng clean

- ct-ng distclean (Be careful; see the following text.)

The ct-ng clean command will usually be enough, forcing the next build to start fresh. Any downloaded files and configuration will remain and are reused.

The ct-ng distclean command is much more drastic, since it removes all of the downloaded content *and your configuration files*. I copied the .config file to .config.bak and discovered to my horror that .config.bak had been removed! So if you back up the .config file, copy it *outside* the current directory for safety.

Above all, keep your head. It's difficult to troubleshoot these issues if you feel time pressure or get angry over the time invested. When under time pressure, leave it for another day when you can deal with it leisurely and thoughtfully. Each redo takes considerable time. Wherever possible, eliminate the guesswork.

With each problem, take a deep breath, patiently look for clues, and pay attention to the details in the error messages. Remember that line in the movie *Apollo 13* : "Work the problem, people!"

CHAPTER 7

■ ■ ■

Cross-Compiling the Kernel

While normally not possible on embedded platforms, it *is* possible to build kernels on your Raspberry Pi with its luxurious root file system. Despite this, cross-compiling on desktop systems is preferred for faster compile times. This chapter examines the procedure for building your Raspbian kernel.

It is assumed that you have the cross-compiler tools and environment ready. Either the tool set built in Chapter 6 or an installed prebuilt tool chain will do. In this chapter, I assume that the cross-compiler prefix is as follows (ending in a hyphen):

/opt/x-tools/arm-unknown-linux-gnueabi/bin/arm-unknown-linux-gnueabi-

Substitute as appropriate, if your tools are installed differently.

Image Tools

According to the "RPi Buying Guide" from eLinux.org, "The way the memory addresses are arranged in the Broadcom SoC, you will need to prepare the compiled image for use." Consequently, an image tool must be used so that the built kernel image can be modified for booting by the Raspberry Pi.

■ **Note** You can read more of the "RPi Buying Guide" at http://s3.amazonaws.com/ szmanuals/8d4eb934fa27c2cbecd2a7f3b6922848.

Let's begin by creating and changing to a work directory:

```
$ mkdir ~/work
$ cd ~/work
```

The tools can be downloaded from here:

```
$ wget https://github.com/raspberrypi/tools/archive/master.tar.gz
```

They can also be fetched from the Git repository:

```
$ git clone --depth 1 git@github.com:raspberrypi/tools.git
```

Save time with the –depth 1 option to avoid downloading older versions that you are uninterested in. The git command will produce a subdirectory named tools. After git has completed, the following additional git steps are recommended:

```
$ rm -fr ./tools/.git       # Delete unneeded .git subdirectory
$ mv tools tools-master     # Rename for consistency in this chapter
$ tar czvf master.tar.gz    # create master.tar.gz as if we downloaded it
```

Whether you simply downloaded master.tar.gz or created it in the preceding step (after using git), unpack the tarball into /opt as follows:

```
$ cd /opt
$ sudo tar xzf ~/work/master.tar.gz
```

This creates the subdirectory /opt/tools-master.

■ **Note**   If you have trouble using git from VirtualBox, there may be networking issues involved (reconfiguration may correct this). The simplest workaround is to simply use git outside VirtualBox and upload the master.tar.gz file with scp.

If you need to save space and you don't need to use the other tools included, remove them:

```
$ cd /opt/tools-master
$ ls
arm-bcm2708  configs  mkimage  pkg  sysidk  usbboot
```

If you are using the cross-compiler from Chapter 6, you won't need the arm-bcm2708 subdirectory:

```
$ cd /opt/tools-master
$ sudo rm -fr arm-bcm2708
```

To use the image tool, you'll need Python installed, so install it now, if needed.

Download Kernel

The first thing needed is the Raspbian kernel sources. If you want the "bleeding edge" in development, the git command is the best way to acquire the source code.

While you could clone the entire Linux project, this will result in a long download. The following method is suggested as a quick way to obtain the kernel release of interest from git (change 3.10.y to the release that you want to fetch):

```
$ mkdir ~/work/linux
$ cd ~/work/linux
$ git init
$ git fetch -depth 1 git@github.com:raspberrypi/linux.git \
      rpi-3.10.y:refs/remotes/origin/rpi-3.10.y
$ git checkout origin/rpi-3.10.y
```

The source tarball can be fetched more easily with the wget command. Here is an example download:

```
$ wget https://github.com/raspberrypi/linux/archive/rpi-3.10.y.tar.gz
```

If you get an error message about an untrusted certificate (ERROR: The certificate of 'github.com' is not trusted), add the –no-check-certificate option:

```
$ wget --no-check-certificate \
  https://github.com/raspberrypi/linux/archive/rpi-3.10.y.tar.gz
```

In this chapter, I assume that you have downloaded the tarball. Once the download is complete, unpack the sources somewhere convenient. I also assume that you're going to use ~/work/rasp as your working directory:

```
$ mkdir -p ~/work/rasp
$ cd ~/work/rasp
$ tar xzf ~/rpi-3.10.y.tar.gz
```

This should leave you a subdirectory named rpi-3.10.y that you can change to the following:

```
$ cd ~/work/rasp/linux-rpi-3.10.y
```

Edit Makefile

It is possible to put the ARCH= and CROSS-COMPILE= definitions on the make command line like this:

```
$ make ARCH=arm CROSS-COMPILE=/opt/x-tools/arm-unknown-\
linux-gnueabi/bin/arm-unknown-linux-gnueabi-
```

However, this is tedious and error prone. You could use an alias or some other workaround, but the best approach is probably just to edit these parameters in the top-level Makefile.

Using an editor of your choice, look for a line in the top-level Makefile that starts with ARCH=, as shown here:

```
ARCH            ?= $ (SUBARCH)
CROSS_COMPILE   ?= $ (CONFIG_CROSS_COMPILE:"%"=%)
```

The safest thing to do is to duplicate these pair of lines and comment out the first pair, keeping them around in their original form. Then modify the second pair as shown:

```
#ARCH            ?= $ (SUBARCH)
#CROSS_COMPILE   ?= $ (CONFIG_CROSS_COMPILE:"%"=%)

ARCH            ?= arm
CROSS_COMPILE   ?= \
  /opt/x-tools/arm-unknown-linux-gnueabi/bin/arm-unknown-linux-gnueabi-
```

The CROSS_COMPILE prefix should match everything up to but not including the command name gcc shown next (edited to fit). If you've not already done so, edit the PATH variable so that the cross-compiler tools are searched first:

```
PATH="/opt/x-tools/arm-unknown-linux-gnueabi/bin:$PATH"
```

Now verify that your compiler is being located:

```
$ type arm-unknown-linux-gnueabi-gcc
arm-unknown-linux-gnueabi-gcc is hashed \
(/opt/x-tools/arm-unknown-linux-gnueabi/bin/arm-unknown-linux-gnueabi-gcc)
```

make mrproper

In theory, this step shouldn't be necessary. But the kernel developers want you to do it anyway, in case something was accidentally left out of place. Keep in mind that this step also removes the .config file. So if you need to keep it, make a copy of it.

```
$ make mrproper
```

▓ **Caution**   The command make mrproper cleans up everything, including your kernel .config file. You may want to copy .config to .config.bak.

Kernel Config

Before building your kernel, you need a configuration. The downloaded kernel source does not include your Pi's kernel settings. If you want to build the kernel with the same configuration as the one you are using, grab your configuration from your running Pi:

```
$ scp pi@rasp:/proc/config.gz .
```

Then uncompress the configuration and move it into place:

```
$ gunzip <config.gz >~/work/rasp/linux-rpi-3.10.y/.config
```

Alternatively, because there may be new options that were not used by your old kernel, you may want to start with a fresh set of default options for your kernel. Copying these defaults will give you a good starting point from which to proceed (assuming the directory ~/work/rasp/linux-rpi-3.10.y):

```
$ cp ./arch/arm/configs/bcmrpi_defconfig .config
```

At this point, you can modify the configuration, but for your first build, I suggest you leave it as is. Once you get a successful build and run of the kernel, you can go back with confidence and make changes. Otherwise, if the new kernel fails, you won't know whether it was the kernel, your build procedure, or the configuration that you chose.

If you downloaded your kernel from the Git repositoryfail if you copied the bcmrpi_defconfig configuration. The reason is that some of the configured modules may not be fully developed (or undergoing changes), but are enabled in the configuration for testing. For example, if an IPTables module fails to compile, you may need to disable it in the configuration. If the option is difficult to find in the menu (see make menuconfig next), it is an accepted practice to just edit the .config file. Things are often easier to find with the editor.

make menuconfig

The first time around, you should start make menuconfig and then just exit. When you decide later that you need to make configuration changes, you can either use the menu-driven approach here or edit the .config file directly. The menu-driven approach is usually best since it can guide you through the process:

```
$ make menuconfig
```

make

Now that the configuration has been established, start the build process. If you hadn't planned on making configuration changes, you might still be prompted with some configuration questions. To proceed without configuration changes, simply press Enter to accept the existing value for the parameter.

```
$ make
```

The build process takes a fair bit of time. On a MacBook Pro using an Intel i7 processor, hosting Ubuntu in VirtualBox, the process takes about 40 minutes to complete. You mileage will vary.

Next, build the modules for the kernel:

```
$ make modules
```

Now you are ready to install the new kernel and its modules.

■ **Tip**   If your /tmp file system is not large enough for the build, you can direct the temporary files to another directory. For example, to use ./tmp in your work area:

```
$ mkdir ./tmp
```

```
$ export TMPDIR="$PWD/tmp"
```

Prepare Kernel Image

In the subdirectory arch/arm/boot/zImage is your built kernel image:

```
$ cd ~/work/rasp/linux-rpi-3.10.y/arch/arm/boot
$ ls -l zImage
-rwxr-xr-x  1  wwg  wwg      3696136  2014-06-22  13:58  zImage
```

Now let's prepare an image that can be booted by the Raspberry Pi.

The image tool seems to need to run from its own directory (otherwise, it is unable to locate the boot-uncompressed.txt file). So change to the image tool's directory and run it from there. It will create the file kernel.img in that directory, so make sure you have permissions there:

```
$ cd /opt/tools-master/mkimage
$ python /opt/tools-master/mkimage/imagetool-uncompressed.py \
     ~/work/rasp/linux-rpi-3.10.y/arch/arm/boot/zImage
$ ls -l
total 3160
```

```
-rw-rw-r--  1 root root      157 May   8 08:14 args-uncompressed.txt
-rw-rw-r--  1 root root      201 May   8 08:14 boot-uncompressed.txt
-rw-rw-r--  1 root root    32768 Jun  24 08:28 first32k.bin
-rwxrwxr-x  1 root root      822 May   8 08:14 imagetool-uncompressed.py
-rw-r--r--  1 root root  3187280 Jun  24 08:28 kernel.img
```

From this, we see that it creates file kernel.img, which is 3,187,280 bytes in size.

Install Kernel Image

Here I assume that you have the SD card mounted on your desktop, rather than in
VirtualBox. The SD card can be mounted in VirtualBox, but this takes some special care
and additional effort. See the "VirtualBox Mount of SD Card" section at the end of the
chapter (if this works for you, this will be more convenient).

With your SD card mounted, you can change out your kernel. It is recommended that
you rename the original kernel.img file in case you want to reinstate it later. On the Mac,
the session might look something like this:

```
$ cd /Volumes/Untitled/       # Where the SD card is mounted
$ ls
bootcode.bin     config.txt      issue.txt        kernel_emergency.img
cmdline.txt      fixup.dat       kernel.img       start.elf
config.bak       fixup_cd.dat    kernel_cutdown.img start_cd.elf
$ mv kernel.img kernel.orig
```

Once the original kernel is safely renamed on the SD card, you can copy the new
kernel onto it:

```
$ scp wwg@osx-rpi:/opt/tools-master/mkimage/kernel.img /Volumes/Untitled/.
wwg@osx-rpi's password:
kernel.img         100%  2665KB    2.6MB/s   00:00
$ sync
```

Here I transferred the prepared image using scp, from VirtualBox machine osx-rpi,
installing the new kernel as kernel.img. You may be able to boot the new kernel without
updating the modules (obviously, the new modules will not be available). Once you
boot up your Pi with the new kernel, then using scp you should be able to copy your new
module's tarball to it (see the "Modules" section later). Try booting the new kernel and
log in to check it (long lines edited):

```
$ ssh pi@rasp
...
$ dmesg | head
...
```

```
[0.000000] Linux version 3.10.38 (wwg@osx-xpi) \
            (gcc version 4.8.2 20130603 (prerelease) \
              (crosstool -NG 1.19.0)) \
            #3 PREEMPT Mon Jun 23 22:26:50 EST 2014
...
```

Here we have confirmation that the kernel was built by wwg@osx-xpi (on VirtualBox), using the crosstool-NG development tools and built on June 23. This is confirmation that the kernel is the new one that was installed. Next, of course, the modules need to be installed.

Boot Failure

If you see the initial colored flash screen remain on the console, this indicates that the kernel.img file failed to load/start.[43]

Modules

The modules need to be staged somewhere, so you can transfer them to the Pi's root file system (on the SD card). Here I'll stage them in ~/work/modules. Specify the full pathname to the staging directory by using the INSTALL_MOD_PATH variable:

```
$ mkdir -p ~/work/modules
$ make INSTALL_MOD_PATH=$HOME/work/modules modules_install
```

Note that $HOME is safer than the tilde (~) in the make command, since the shell may not substitute it properly. The bash shell, version 4.3.8, does seem to handle the tilde, however.

After this install step completes, you will have a subtree of kernel modules deposited there. These files now need to be installed in the Pi's root file system. Either mount the Pi's root file system under Linux, or use the existing kernel on the Pi itself. The following shows how the modules are put into a tar file for transport to the Pi:

```
$ cd ~/work/modules
$ tar czf modules.tar.gz .
$ tar tzf modules.tar.gz | head -4
. /
. /modules.tar.gz
. /lib/
. /lib/modules/
$ scp modules.tar.gz pi@rasp:.
```

On the Raspberry Pi, you can install it:

```
$ tar tzf modules.tar.gz | head-7
. /
. /modules.tar.gz
. /lib/
. /lib/modules/
. /lib/modules/3.2.27/
. /lib/modules/3.2.27/modules.symbols.bin
. /lib/modules/3.2.27/modules.usbmap
$ cd  /
$ sudo tar xzf ~/modules.tar.gz
```

With the new modules installed, reboot your new kernel. Once the Pi boots up, log in and check whether any modules got loaded:

```
$ lsmod
Module       Size       Used   by
snd_bcm2835  16292      0
...
```

Firmware

From time to time, you should check to see whether new firmware is available. This code is available in binary form only. There are always two versions of the firmware available:[35]

> *Master*: The current firmware used in Raspbian

> *Next*: The firmware in development, which provides GPU updates

Depending on your needs, choose one of the following:

```
$ wget--no-check-certificate\
  https://github.com/raspberrypi/firmware/archive/master.tar.gz
```

```
$ wget--no-check-certificate\
  https://github.com/raspberrypi/firmware/archive/next.tar.gz
```

Of particular interest is the bootcode.bin firmware file. There are other files like the *.dat files. It is unclear when these dat files should be replaced. These may depend on the release of the Raspbian Linux kernel.

```
$ cd ./firmware-master/boot
$ ls -l
total 37248
-rw-r--r--   ..     18693  26 Jan 14:31   COPYING.linux
-rw-r--r--   ..      1447  26 Jan 14:31   LICENCE.broadcom
-rw-r--r--   ..     17764  26 Jan 14:31   bootcode.bin
-rw-r--r--   ..      5735  26 Jan 14:31   fixup.dat
-rw-r--r--   ..      2260  26 Jan 14:31   fixup_cd.dat
-rw-r--r--   ..      8502  26 Jan 14:31   fixup_x.dat
-rw-r--r--   ..   2800968  26 Jan 14:31   kernel.img
-rw-r--r--   ..   9609864  26 Jan 14:31   kernel_emergency.img
-rw-r--r--   ..   2539540  26 Jan 14:31   start.elf
-rw-r--r--   ..    569016  26 Jan 14:31   start_cd.elf
-rw-r--r--   ..   3472580  26 Jan 14:31   start_x.elf
```

If you think you need a firmware update, copy from this subdirectory to your Raspberry Pi's /boot directory.

VirtualBox Mount of SD Card

All this shuffling images around remotely using scp is a nuisance, but it gets the job done. If you are running VirtualBox, you may find that you can mount the SD card directly. This allows you to more easily update the SD card file systems, including the modules and firmware. I'll be showing the VirtualBox procedure for a Mac, but the process is similar for Windows.

The first step on the Mac is to determine which disk device the SD card is assigned to:

```
$ diskutil list
```

In my case, the SD card showed up as /dev/disk2 (this is obvious because it wasn't there prior to inserting the SD card).

Next you need to make sure that any mounted file systems from that SD card are unmounted (the Mac likes to automount everything it can). Using the diskutil command, unmount all file systems mounted from /dev/disk2:

```
$ diskutil unmountDisk /dev/disk2
```

Finally (for the Mac), you need to grant permissions to VirtualBox to use the raw device. Since VirtualBox likely runs under your own login, you need to grant permissions to it. I'll use the lazy approach here, to grant permissions to everyone on the device (the device will go away as soon as it is removed anyway):

```
$ sudo chmod 0666 /dev/disk2
```

Note that once you remove the SD card, and later insert it, you will need to repeat this step.

Next, you will need to locate the VBoxManage command. On the Mac you will find it here (Windows users may find it in C:\Program Files\Sun):

```
$ cd /Applications/VirtualBox.app/Contents/MacOS
```

You can either add that directory to your current PATH, or simply change to that directory. Then use the VBoxManage command to create a control file (*.vmdk). This control file informs VirtualBox how to access that raw device (place the *.vmdk wherever you find it convenient):

```
$ sudo VBoxManage internalcommands createrawvmdk \
    -filename /Volumes/VirtualBox/sddisk.vmdk \
    -rawdisk /dev/disk2
```

Now enter your VirtualBox console and open the storage settings. Click the Add Hard Disk icon and select the control file you created (in the example, it was created on /Volumes/VirtualBox/sddisk.vmdk). Make sure you add this device after your current boot device. Otherwise, VirtualBox will try to boot from your SD card instead.

After starting VirtualBox, you should see your new devices under Linux. In my case, the SD card devices showed up as /dev/sdb (entire SD card), /dev/sdb1 (partition 1), and /dev/sdb2 (partition 2). With this success, it is now possible to mount these partitions after creating mount points (I used ~/mnt1 and ~/mnt2):

```
$ sudo mount /dev/sdb1 ~/mnt1
$ sudo mount /dev/sdb2 ~/mnt2
```

Now you can list those mount points to see the Raspberry Pi file system content. This access makes it an easy matter to install your kernel:

```
$ cd /opt/tools-master/mkimage
$ sudo mv ~/mnt1/kernel.img ~/mnt1/kernel.orig   # Rename original kernel
$ sudo dd if=kernel.img ~/mnt1/kernel.img        # Install new kernel image
```

Likewise, you can now update the kernel modules:

```
$ cd ~/mnt2                                  # Raspberry Pi' Root file system
$ tar xzvf ~/work/modules/modules.tar.gz     # Unpack into ~/mnt2/lib
```

With the modifications completed, change out of the file system (to unbusy them) and unmount them:

```
$ cd ~
$ sudo umount ~/mnt1
$ sudo umount ~/mnt2
```

If you are hosting VirtualBox on a Mac, the Mac will automount the first partition the moment that VirtualBox closes the SD card device. So be sure to undo that before pulling the SD card out (to prevent any file system corruption). You can use the Mac's diskutil to do this for you:

```
$ diskutil unmountDisk /dev/disk2
```

APPENDIX A

Glossary

AC
Alternating current

Amps
Amperes

ATAG
ARM tags, though now used by boot loaders for other architectures

AVC
Advanced Video Coding (MPEG-4)

AVR
Wikipedia states that "it is commonly accepted that AVR stands for Alf (Egil Bogen) and Vegard (Wollan)'s RISC processor."

BCD
Binary-coded decimal

Brick
To accidently render a device unusable by making changes to it

CEA
Consumer Electronics Association

cond
Condition variable

CPU
Central processing unit

CRC
Cyclic redundancy check, a type of hash for error detection

CVT
Coordinated Video Timings standard (replaces GTF)

daemon
A Unix process that services requests in the background

DC
Direct current

DCD
> RS-232 data carrier detect

DCE
> RS-232 data communications equipment

Distro
> A specific distribution of Linux software

DLNA
> Digital Living Network Alliance, whose purpose is to enable sharing of digital media between multimedia devices

DMM
> Digital multimeter

DMT
> Display Monitor Timing standard

DPI
> Display Pixel Interface (a parallel display interface)

DPVL
> Digital Packet Video Link

DSI
> Display Serial Interface

DSR
> RS-232 data set ready

DTE
> RS-232 data terminal equipment

DTR
> RS-232 data terminal ready

ECC
> Error-correcting code

EDID
> Extended display identification data

EEPROM
> Electrically erasable programmable read-only memory

EMMC
> External mass media controller

Flash
> Similar to EEPROM, except that large blocks must be entirely rewritten in an update operation

FFS
> Flash file system

FIFO
First in, first out

FSP
Flash storage processor

FTL
Flash translation layer

FUSE
Filesystem in Userspace (File system in USErspace)

GNU
GNU is not Unix

GPIO
General-purpose input/output

GPU
Graphics processing unit

GTF
Generalized Timing Formula

H.264
MPEG-4 Advanced Video Coding (AVC)

H-Bridge
An electronic circuit configuration that allows voltage to be reversed across the load

HDMI
High-Definition Multimedia Interface

HID
Human interface device

I2C
Two-wire interface invented by Philips

IC
Integrated circuit

IDE
Integrated development environment

IR
Infrared

ISP
Image Sensor Pipeline

JFFS2
Journalling Flash File System 2

LCD
Liquid-crystal display

LED
Light-emitting diode

mA
Milliamperes, a measure of current flow

MCU
Microcontroller unit

MMC
MultiMedia Card

MISO
Master in, slave out

MOSI
Master out, slave in

MTD
Memory technology device

mutex
Mutually exclusive

NTSC
National Television System Committee (analog TV signal standard)

PAL
Phase Alternating Line (analog TV signal standard)

PC
Personal computer

PCB
Printed circuit board

PLL
Phase-locked loop

PoE
Power over Ethernet (supplying power over an Ethernet cable)

POSIX
Portable Operating System Interface (for Unix)

pthreads
POSIX threads

PWM
Pulse-width modulation

Pxe
Preboot execution environment, usually referencing booting by network

RAM
Random-access memory

RI
    RS-232 ring indicator

RISC
    Reduced instruction set computer

RH
    Relative humidity

ROM
    Read-only memory

RPi
    Raspberry Pi

RS-232
    Recommended standard 232 (serial communications)

RTC
    Real-time clock

SBC
    Single-board computer

SD
    Secure Digital Association memory card

SDIO
    SD card input/output interface

SDRAM
    Synchronous dynamic random-access memory

SoC
    System on a chip

SMPS
    Switched-mode power supply

SPI
    Serial Peripheral Interface (bus)

Stick parity
    Mark or space parity, where the bit is constant

TWI
    Two-wire interface

UART
    Universal asynchronous receiver/transmitter

USB
    Universal Serial Bus

V3D
    Video for 3D

VAC
Volts AC

VESA
Video Electronics Standards Association

VFS
Virtual file system

VNC
Virtual Network Computing

V$_{SB}$
ATX standby voltage

YAFFS
Yet Another Flash File System

APPENDIX B

▓ ▓ ▓

Power Standards

The following table references the standard ATX power supply voltages, regulation (tolerance), and voltage ranges.[15]

The values listed here for the +5 V and +3.3 V supplies are referenced in Chapter 2 of *Raspberry Pi Hardware Reference* (Apress, 2014) as a basis for acceptable power supply ranges. When the BroadCom power specifications become known, they should be used instead.

Supply (Volts)	Tolerance		Minimum	Maximum	Ripple (Peak to Peak)
+5 V	±5%	± 0.25 V	+4.75 V	+5.25 V	50 mV
-5 V	+10%	±0.50 V	−4.50 V	−5.50 V	50 mV
+12 V	±5%	±0.60 V	+11.40 V	+12.60 V	120 mV
-12 V	±10%	±1.2 V	−10.8 V	−13.2 V	120 mV
+3.3 V	±5%	±0.165 V	+3.135 V	+3.465 V	50 mV
+5 V_{SB}	±5%	±0.25 V	+4.75 V	+5.25 V	50 mV

APPENDIX C

Raspbian apt Commands

This appendix highlights the usage of commonly used package management commands under Raspbian Linux.

List Available Packages

```
$ apt-cache pkgnames
tesseract-ocr-epo
pipenightdreams
openoffice.org-l10n-mn
mumudvb
tbb-examples
libsvm-java
libsalck3-dev
libboost-timer1.50-dev
snort-rules-default
freediams-doc-fr
...
```

List Installed Packages

```
$ dpkg -l
Desired=Unknown/Install/Remove/Purge/Hold
| Status=Not/Inst/Conf-files/Unpacked/halF-conf/Half-inst/trig-aWait/
  Trig-pend
|/ Err?=(none)/Reinst-required (Status,Err: uppercase=bad)
```

```
||/ Name           Version          Architecture    Description
+++ -============  -=============   -=============-  ==========================
ii  adduser        3.113+nmu3       all             add and remove users
                                                    and groups
ii  alsa-base      1.0.25+2+nmu2    all             ALSA driver
                                                    configuration files
ii  alsa-utils     1.0.25-3         armhf           Utilities for configuring
                                                    and \ using ALSA
ii  apt            0.9.7.6+rpi1     armhf           commandline package manager
ii  apt-utils      0.9.7.6+rpi1     armhf           package managment related \
                                                    utility programs
```

List Files for Package

```
$dpkg -L apt
/.
/etc
/etc/cron.daily
/etc/cron.daily/apt
/etc/logrotate.d
/etc/logrotate.d/apt
/etc/apt
/etc/apt/apt.conf.d
/etc/apt/apt.conf.d/01autoremove
/etc/apt/preferences.d
...
```

Perform Package Search

```
$ apt-cache search gnuplot
...
devscripts - scripts to make the life of a Debian Package maintainer easier
gnuplot - Command -line driven interactive plotting program
gnuplot-doc - Command -line driven interactive plotting program. Doc-package
gnuplot-mode - Yet another Gnuplot mode for Emacs
gnuplot-nox - Command-line driven interactive plotting program. No-X package
gnuplot-qt - Command-line driven interactive plotting program. QT-package
gnuplot-x11 - Command-line driven interactive plotting program. X-package
libchart-gnuplot -perl - module for generating two - and
three-dimensional plots
libgnuplot-ocaml -dev - OCaml interface to the gnuplot utility
libgnuplot-ruby - Transitional package for ruby-gnuplot
libgnuplot-ruby1 .8 - Transitional package for ruby-gnuplot
```

```
libgraphics-gnuplotif-perl - dynamic Perl interface to gnuplot
libploticus0 - script driven business graphics library
libploticus0-dev - Development files for the ploticus library
...
```

Install a Package

```
$ sudo apt-get install gnuplot-x11
Reading package lists...
Building dependency tree...
Reading state information...
The following extra packages will be installed:
    libglu1-mesa liblua5.1-0 libwxbase2.8-0 libwxgtk2.8-0
Suggested packages:
    gnuplot-doc libgnomeprintui2.2-0
The following NEW packages will be installed:
    gnuplot-x11 libglu1-mesa liblua5.1-0  libwxbase2.8-0  libwxgtk2.8-0
0 upgraded, 5 newly installed, 0 to remove and 107 not upgraded.
Need to get 4,967 kB of archives.
After this operation, 12.4 MB of additional disk space will be used.
Do you want to continue [Y/n]? y
Get:1 http :// mirrordirector.raspbian.org/raspbian/ wheezy/main libglu1-
mesa armhf 8.0.5-3 [152 kB]
Get:2 http :// mirrordirector.raspbian.org/raspbian/ wheezy/main liblua5.1-0
armhf 5.1.5-4 [145 kB]
Get:3 http :// mirrordirector.raspbian.org/raspbian/ wheezy/main
libwxbase2.8-0 armhf 2.8.12.1-12 [599 kB]
Get:4 http :// mirrordirector.raspbian.org/raspbian/ wheezy/main
libwxgtk2.8-0 armhf 2.8.12.1-12 [3 ,011 kB]
Get:5 http :// mirrordirector.raspbian.org/raspbian/ wheezy/main gnuplot-x11
armhf 4.6.0-8 [1 ,059 kB]
Fetched 4,967 kB in 12s (408 kB/s)
Selecting previously unselected package libglu1-mesa:armhf.
(Reading database ... 60788 files and directories currently installed .)

Unpacking libglu1 -mesa:armhf (from .../libglu1-mesa_8.0.5-3 _armhf.deb) ...
Selecting previously unselected package liblua5.1-0: armhf.
Unpacking liblua5.1-0: armhf (from .../liblua5.1-0_5.1.5-4 _armhf.deb) ...
Selecting previously unselected package libwxbase2.8-0: armhf.
Unpacking libwxbase2.8-0: armhf (from .../libwxbase2.8-0_2.8.12.1-12_armhf.
deb) ...
Selecting previously unselected package libwxgtk2.8-0: armhf.
Unpacking libwxgtk2.8-0: armhf (from .../libwxgtk2.8-0_2.8.12.1-12_armhf.
deb) ...
Selecting previously unselected package gnuplot-x11.
```

```
Unpacking gnuplot-x11 (from .../gnuplot-x11_4.6.0-8_armhf.deb) ...
Processing triggers for menu ...
Processing triggers for man-db ...
Setting up libglu1-mesa:armhf (8.0.5-3) ...
Setting up liblua5.1-0:armhf (5.1.5-4) ...
Setting up libwxbase2.8-0:armhf (2.8.12.1-12) ...
Setting up libwxgtk2.8-0:armhf (2.8.12.1-12) ...
Setting up gnuplot-x11 (4.6.0-8) ...
Processing triggers for menu ...
$
```

Remove a Package

```
# apt-get remove pkg_name
# apt-get purge pkg_name
```

Install Updates

```
# apt-get update
```

Upgrade

```
# apt-get upgrade
```

Obtain Kernel Sources

```
$ wget --no-check-certificate \
  -O raspberrypi-linux-3.6.11.tar.gz \
  http://github.com/raspberrypi/linux/tarball/rpi-3.6.y
```

APPENDIX D

■ ■ ■

ARM Compile Options

For ARM platform compiles, the following site makes compiler option recommendations: http://elinux.org/RPi_Software.

The site states the following:

- The gcc compiler flags that produce the most optimal code for the Raspberry Pi are as follows:

    - -Ofast -mfpu=vfp -mfloat-abi=hard -march=armv6zk -mtune=arm1176jzf-s

- For some programs, -Ofast may produce compile errors. In these cases, -O3 or -O2 should be used instead.

- -mcpu=arm1176jzf-s can be used in place of -march=armv6zk -mtune=arm1176jzf-s.

APPENDIX E

■ ■ ■

Mac OS X Tips

This appendix offers a couple of tips pertaining to Raspberry Pi SD card operations under Mac OS X. Figure E-1 shows an SD card reader and a built-in card slot being used.

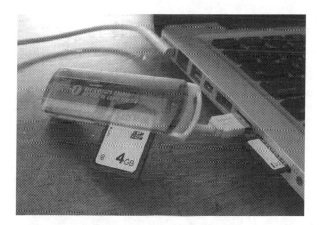

Figure E-1. *USB card reader and MacBook Pro SD slot*

The one problem that gets in the way of working with Raspberry Pi images on SD cards is the automounting of partitions when the card is inserted. This, of course, can be disabled, but the desktop user will find this inconvenient. So you need a way to turn it off, when needed.

Another problem that occurs is determining the OS X device name for the card. When copying disk images, you need to be certain of the device name! Both of these problems are solved using the Mac diskutil command (found in /usr/sbin/diskutil).

■ **Caution**   Copying to the wrong device on your Mac can destroy all of your files. Be afraid!

Before inserting your SD cards, do the following:

```
$ diskutil list
/dev/disk0
#:                   TYPE NAME                  SIZE         IDENTIFIER
0:      GUID_partition_scheme           *750.2 GB          disk0
1:      EFI                              209.7 MB          disk0s1
2:      Apple_HFS Macintosh HD          749.3 GB           disk0s2
3:      Apple_Boot Recovery HD          650.0 MB           disk0s3
```

Check the mounts:

```
$ mount
/dev/disk0s2 on / (hfs, NFS exported, local, journaled)
...
```

Insert the SD card:

```
$ diskutil list
/dev/disk0
#:                     TYPE NAME                SIZE         IDENTIFIER
0:      GUID_partition_scheme           *750.2 GB          disk0
1:                          EFI          209.7 MB          disk0s1
2:    Apple_HFS   Macintosh HD          749.3 GB           disk0s2
3:    Apple_Boot   Recovery HD          650.0 MB           disk0s3
/dev/disk1
#:                   TYPE NAME                  SIZE         IDENTIFIER
0:      FDisk_partition_scheme            *3.9 GB          disk1
1:            Windows_FAT_32             58.7 MB           disk1s1
2:                      Linux             3.8 GB           disk1s2
```

Unmount any automounted partitions for disk1:

```
$ diskutil unmountDisk /dev/disk1
Unmount of all volumes on disk1 was successful
$
```

Likewise, insert the destination SD card and use diskutil to get its device name (mine was /dev/disk2). Unmount all file systems that may have been automounted for it (diskutil unmountDisk).

At this point, you can perform a file system image copy:

```
$ dd if=/dev/disk1 of=/dev/disk2 bs=1024k
3724+0 records in 3724+0 records out
3904897024 bytes transferred in 2571.524357 secs (1518515 bytes/sec)
$
```

Index

Get the eBook for only $10!

Now you can take the weightless companion with you anywhere, anytime. Your purchase of this book entitles you to 3 electronic versions for only $10.

This Apress title will prove so indispensible that you'll want to carry it with you everywhere, which is why we are offering the eBook in 3 formats for only $10 if you have already purchased the print book.

Convenient and fully searchable, the PDF version enables you to easily find and copy code—or perform examples by quickly toggling between instructions and applications. The MOBI format is ideal for your Kindle, while the ePUB can be utilized on a variety of mobile devices.

Go to www.apress.com/promo/tendollars to purchase your companion eBook.